The Cambrian Mountains landscape

A landscape assessment prepared
by Land Use Consultants
for the Countryside Commission

Published by:
Countryside Commission
John Dower House
Crescent Place
Cheltenham GL50 3RA
© Countryside Commission 1990

Distributed by:
Countryside Commission Publications
19/23 Albert Road
Manchester M19 2EQ
CCP 293
Price £6.50

Contents

Figures

British Library Cataloguing in Publication Data
The Cambrian Mountains landscape. – CCP: 293
1. Wales. Cambrian Mountains. Landscape
I. Land Use Consultants. II Great Britain, Countryside Commission.
719.09429
ISBN 0–86170–248–4

Designed and produced by The Edge – Cheltenham

Preface

This report covers an area that was designated, but not confirmed, as a national park in 1972, and which became an Environmentally Sensitive Area (ESA) in 1987/88. It is one of a series, published by the Countryside Commission, describing the character and value of important landscapes in England and Wales. Each report has different origins and therefore differs in its content and emphasis. The first two titles – *The New Forest landscape* and *The Blackdown Hills landscape* – attempted to evoke the special qualities of those particular landscapes in a way that would be of general and popular appeal, and to make a clear statement about their importance.

In the case of the Cambrian Mountains, the report is based on work carried out for the Countryside Commission specifically to develop and test a practical method for systematic large-scale landscape assessment. A detailed description and assessment of the landscape was produced, at a level of detail that could influence thinking on landscape conservation and management issues such as forestry, agricultural roads and moorland reclamation.

For this reason, this report is more technical than its predecessors and examines in greater detail variation within the landscape, rather than overall character. It also includes information about the method of assessment used (see Appendix 1). However, the last two chapters also detail the way in which the landscape is perceived and the importance attached to it.

This assessment therefore stands as a clear statement of the significance of this very important area of Welsh landscape as well as a detailed examination of the variation within it.

The original landscape assessment, aimed mainly at developing the method, was carried out in 1986 for an area then defined as the Mid Wales uplands (see *Mid Wales uplands study*, CCP 177). In 1988 the assessment was extended to include the area newly designated as an ESA, and was put to practical use in developing the landscape and receational aspects of a forestry strategy for the area.

Land Use Consultants

Cover photo: *Plateau tops with moorland in the Elenydd landscape area*

Rhagair

Mae'r adroddiad hwn yn ymwuned â rhanbarth anghysbell ac eang o ucheldir Cymru y mae ei gadwraeth yn fater o bryder ers blynyddoedd lawer i'r Comisiwn Cefn Gwlad. Mae'r bryniau tonnog a gwyrdd rhwng y Dyfi a'r Tywi'n un o ardaloedd lleiaf adnabyddus a lleiaf poblog Cymru. Eithr ceir yno dirwedd sydd mor syfrdanol nes i'r Comisiwn ei dewis ar gyfer prosiect i gynorthwyo yn y gwaith o ddatblygu technegau o asesu tirwedd.

Yr ydym oll yn gwerthfawrogi a choleddu harddwch ein cefn gwlad. Fel y mae'r pwysau i'w newid yn cynyddu – ynghyd â chefnogaeth y cyhoedd dros gadw prydferthwch naturiol a bywyd gwyllt – daw'n fwywy pwysig i ddatblygu dulliau syml o ddadansoddi cymeriad tirwedd. Mae hwnnw'n gam hanfodol tuag at adnabod yr ardaloedd hynny y mae hi fwyaf angenrheidiol i'w cadw.

Cefnogai'r gwaith gwreiddiol ar gyfer yr adroddiad hwn argymhelliad y Comisiwn Cefn Gwlad i'r Llywodraeth y Dylai Mynyddoedd y Canolbarth gael eu dynodi'n Ardal Amgylchedd Arbennig. Gyda'i phenodi'n AAA ym 1987/88 caiff ffermwyr erbyn hyn gymorthdaliadau arbennig i'w helpu i ddiogelu'r glaswellt cwrs, sef nodwedd hanfodol tirwedd y bryniau hyn.

Yn y tymor hir, mae amddiffyn tirweddau mor bwysig yn dibynnu ar well ddealltwriaeth a gwerthfawrogiad ohonynt gan gyhoedd sydd yn ymwybodol o'r sefyllfa. Gobeithio y darllennir yr adroddiad hwn nid yn unig gan amgylchfydwyr proffesiynol, ond hefyd gan eraill sydd yn ceisio ymwybyddiaeth ddyfnach o berfeddwlad Cymru – y rhan honno o fynyddoedd y Canolbarth rhwng y Dyfi a'r Tywi.

Meuric Rees.

Meuric Rees CBE, YH, DL
Cadeirydd, Pwyllgor Cymru
Comisiwn Cefn Gwlad

Foreword

This report is about a remote and extensive part of the Welsh uplands, the conservation of which has for many years been of concern to the Countryside Commission. The rolling green hills between the Dyfi and the Tywi are one of the least known and least populated parts of Wales. But here is a landscape which is so outstanding that the Commission chose it for a project to help develop techniques of landscape assessment.

We all value and cherish the beauty of our countryside. As the pressures for its change grow – along with public support for the conservation of natural beauty and wildlife – it is increasingly important to develop straightforward methods of analysing landscape character. That is the essential step towards identifying those areas which it is most essential to conserve.

The original work for this report supported the Countryside Commission's recommendation to the Government that the Cambrian Mountains should become an Environmentally Sensitive Area (ESA). The subsequent ESA designation in 1987/88 now provides farmers with special incentives to help them to safeguard the rough grassland which is the essential landscape feature of these hills.

In the long term, protection of such vital landscapes lies through their better understanding and appreciation by a well-informed public. I hope that this report will be read not only by environmental professionals but also by others who seek a deeper knowledge of the heartland of Wales – the Cambrian Mountains.

Meuric Rees.

Meuric Rees CBE, JP, DL
Chairman, Committee for Wales
Countryside Commission

Fig 1 Location map

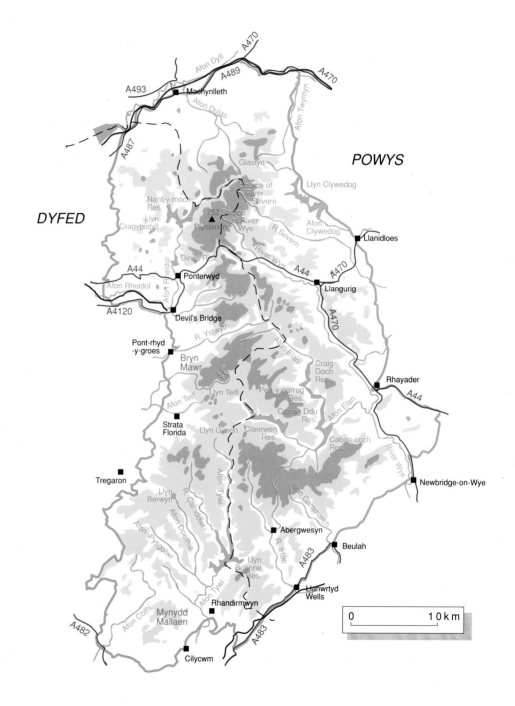

Legend:

Cambrian Mountains ESA boundary

Major roads

Railway

County boundary

Land above 500m

400-500m

Places of interest

0   10 km

1. The nature of the Cambrian Mountains

Introduction

The Cambrian Mountains (Figure 1) form a substantial part of the backbone of Wales, straddling the County Boundary between Dyfed and Powys. The Dyfi Valley divides this upland massif from Cadair Idris to the north, while the next upland area to the south is Mynydd Eppynt. The area has traditionally been referred to as 'the great Welsh desert' because of the characteristic whale-back ridges of uniform upland grassland which, before changes in land use, rolled away into the distance like sand dunes with no visible interruption. The remote, empty and often hostile character of the landscape also creates an illusion of wilderness which is highly valued by those seeking solitude and escape, and is characterised by plateaux, valleys and edges.

Plateaux

The Cambrian Mountains consist mainly of land above an elevation of 300 m (1,000 feet), reaching peaks of 750 m (2,400 feet) in places; but strictly speaking the area is not mountainous. It is more a dissected plateau of soft Silurian rocks, including slates, mudstones and sandstones which form a landscape dominated by rounded hills and undulating plateaux. Limited areas of local protruding inliers of older and harder Ordovician grits cross through the area to the north and south-east and often form a more rugged landscape which includes the Plynlimon massif.

Despite significant changes in land use in recent years, large parts of these rolling central plateaux are still covered in semi-natural upland vegetation (see Figure 2). Much of the moorland is grass moor, with extensive tracts of purple moor grass and mat grass, and fescue grassland on the flanks of the rolling hills and cotton grass on the flat summits. Heather and bilberry communities occur in limited areas in the east on some of the flanks of the Wye Valley, on the summits and valley sides above Rhayader and east of the Elan Valley, in the south-west on Mynydd Mallaen, in the central area on the hills above Cwm Ystwyth and in the north on the escarpment and the plateau top around the lake of Glaslyn. Bracken is prominent especially in eastern areas, in the south-west, and in the north-west and north, particularly on steep slopes and areas of better soil.

It is the high, wild plateau moorlands, rolling away in receding ridges, which are so much a feature of the distinctive Cambrian Mountains landscape.

Valleys

The high plateau moorlands are deeply cut by a number of river valleys and gorges (see Figure 3). The Wye, the Severn, the Elan, the Rheidol, the Ystwyth, the Teifi, the Tywi and the Clywedog all have their sources in the high moorlands. The Wye, the Severn, the Elan and the Clywedog all flow east. In general, the

Forestry, agricultural improvement and construction of farm roads have all brought about major change in the landscape.

rivers flowing to the west are more deeply incised than those to the east, particularly the Rheidol and the Llyfnant in the north-west, the Ystwyth in the west and the Cothi and the middle reaches of the Tywi in the south-west. The Rheidol is a particularly notable example, forming the spectacular and deeply incised gorges in the vicinity of Devil's Bridge and then opening into the broad Vale of Rheidol further west. In the south, the Irfon and its tributaries drain south then east to join the River Wye, carving deep valleys in the plateaux.

Deciduous woodlands are a particular characteristic of a number of the steep-sided valleys. Many have been changed over the years by conifer planting, but a number still remain and are a prominent and attractive feature in the landscape wherever they occur. Notable examples are in the area east of Rhayader and around the Elan Valley, along the northern escarpment, in the Vale of Rheidol, and in the Cothi, Tywi, and Pysgotwr valleys in the south-west. They also occur in agricultural areas around the fringes of the uplands. The valley woods are primarily sessile oak woodland, many of which are also of great value for nature conservation.

These river valleys provide a perfect foil to the exposed moorlands. They are enclosed and sheltered, with the better soils supporting improved pasture, and the steep valley sides clad in deciduous woodland, and they provide a complete contrast to the bleak, open plateaux above.

Edges and escarpments

The other characteristic feature of the Cambrian Mountains occurs where the plateaux drop away to the surrounding areas lying at lower altitudes. Sometimes this transition is gentle and the edges of the plateaux form folded rolling hills, but in the north it is dramatic, with steep moorland escarpments cut by gorges and waterfalls falling away and providing a backdrop to lower hills and woodlands below. The tributaries of the River Dyfi flow off the plateaux over this northern escarpment in a series of spectacular waterfalls.

Both the valleys and parts of the plateau margins include areas of improved pasture. These pastures often form part of a diverse and well-wooded agricultural landscape. The hedgerows are, in general, tall and overgrown. They are made up of hazel and rowan in many places, in combination with other species, and often give the landscape a lush, well-wooded appearance which is often referred to as 'bosky'.

Change in the landscape

These features of open rolling moorland, sheltered wooded valleys and dramatic escarpments and gorges are the traditional features of the landscape of the Cambrian Mountains which has been highly valued and much praised over the years. The past forty years have, however, seen dramatic changes in this traditional landscape. Rivers have been dammed to form major reservoirs at Llyn Brianne and Llyn Clywedog, to add to the existing ones in the Elan Valley; moorland and rough grazing has been improved or reclaimed to provide better quality grazing; and coniferous plantations have replaced broadleaved woodland in valleys and have extended over large areas of plateau moorland. The *Mid Wales uplands study* of 1985 clearly indicated the nature and pace of change since the war, noting that rough pasture had declined from 78 per cent of the area in 1948 to 55 per cent in 1983. Coniferous afforestation accounted for most of this change in the period up to 1978, while land improvement for agriculture has become more significant since then.

Today, forestry plantations are a prominent feature of the landscape, with substantial areas of moorland having been planted in the past forty years. Cultivated and improved land has also become more important. It has always been a feature of the valley bottoms and lower-lying plateau fringe areas, but as agricultural improvement techniques have advanced, more rough grazing has been converted to improved grassland, even at quite high altitude on the moorland plateaux. It seems likely that the rate of reclamation of moorland in the late 1970s and early 1980s was one of the highest in all the upland areas in Britain. As a result of these changes, there is now a mosaic throughout the area of traditional and new landscape features, which interact with the natural landform to create a great range of different types of landscape.

2. Types of landscape in the Cambrian Mountains

Identifying the range of landscape types

The method used in this landscape assessment is described in Appendix 1. Its use resulted in classification of the Cambrian Mountains area into a range of clearly recognisable landscape types based on particular combinations of landform and land cover. Landform is the main determinant of the landscape in this area, and four broad landform divisions provide the initial basis for the classification; namely, upland plateaux, plateau margins, narrow valleys and broad valleys. These broad categories are further divided on the basis of differences in topography and in vegetation and land use, to produce nineteen landscape types which have a distinct character. The distribution of the broad landform divisions and of the nineteen landscape types is shown in Figure 4. The main divisions can be briefly described as follows.

Upland plateaux

The upland plateaux form the heart of the Cambrian Mountains area. The plateau landscapes range from high and irregular peaks and knobs, which rise to 700 m and include Plynlimon Fawr, to extensive plateau tops (450–500 m) and shallow rolling plateaux (300–500 m). These landscapes are typically wild, windswept, remote and covered by rough moorland vegetation. Large areas are only accessible on foot and the moorlands offer extensive 'wilderness' walks with distant panoramic views. There are five upland plateau landscape types.

Plateau margins

The plateau margin landscapes vary from dramatic cliffs and cirques to fragmented hill slopes and saddles. Substantial elevation changes affect the land cover in these areas, which range from windswept upland moor, scree slopes and plantations of sitka spruce at 500 m, to bosky, enclosed farmland at 150 m. The Dulas Scarp in the north and Pont Marteg cirque on the main A44 are highly visible and important landscape features for visitors to the area, but many of the hill slopes and saddles are inaccessible and often less attractive. There are four plateau margin landscape types.

Narrow valleys

The narrow valleys make up the largest proportion of the area. They cover a wide variety of landforms, from gorges and ravines to U-shaped valleys, but they are all upland stream or river corridors, draining directly from the upper plateaux. The land cover variation is also great, ranging from moorland to conifer plantations, and inbye pasture to mixed woodland and thick broadleaved woodland. A number of these valleys have also been flooded to form reservoirs, creating further variety. There are eight narrow valley landscape types.

Broad valleys

The broad valleys include wide river corridors and river confluences. They are characterised by flat valley bottoms with bosky enclosed farm land and settlements. Major roads pass through the valleys, providing the main entry points and access corridors through the area. Valley sides are steep and historically have been wooded. Some broadleaved woodlands remain but many have been cleared for pasture or replaced by coniferous plantations. There are two broad valley landscape types.

Individual landscape types are described in greater detail in the following pages. The distribution of each in the area is shown in the key map, together with a figure showing the extent of each area. A description of the general landscape character is followed by notes on any variations which occur between areas and on access and recreation in each. Key landscape elements and dominant colours are noted, together with a summary of the main descriptive terms used to describe the landscape at the survey stage. Finally, any potentially discordant elements which could have an adverse effect on the character of the landscape are listed. A sketch illustrates the typical character of each landscape. Photographs of all nineteen landscape types are shown in Chapter 3.

Upland plateaux

Plateau margins

Narrow valleys

Broad valleys

The four main landform types.

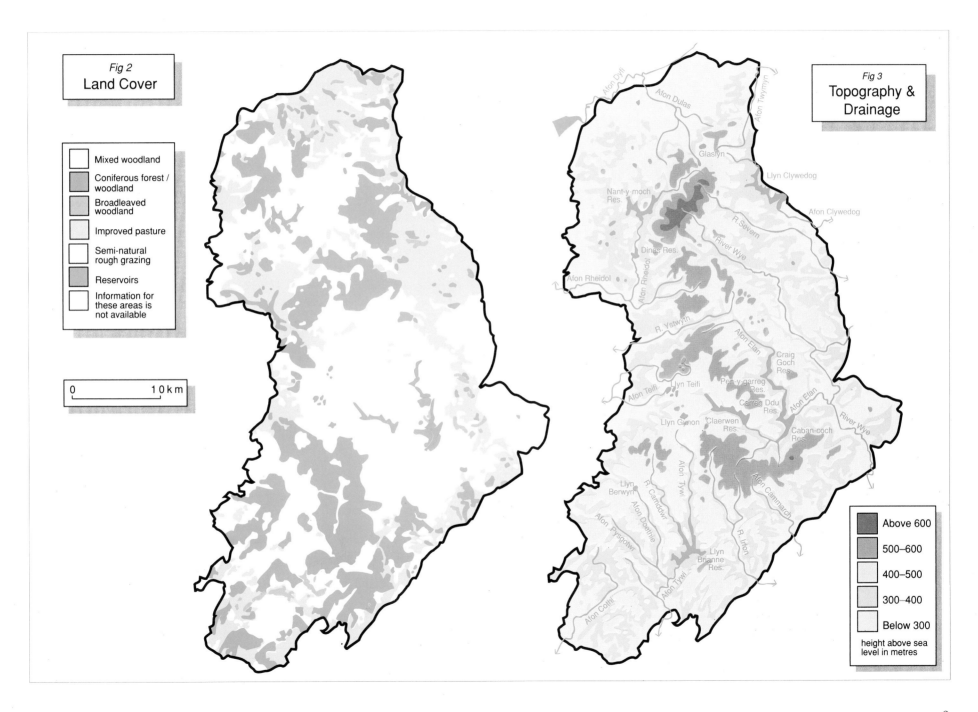

Fig 2
Land Cover

Mixed woodland

Coniferous forest / woodland

Broadleaved woodland

Improved pasture

Semi-natural rough grazing

Reservoirs

Information for these areas is not available

0   10 km

Fig 3
Topography & Drainage

Afon Dyfi

Afon Dulas

Afon Twymyn

Glaslyn

Llyn Clywedog

Nant-y-moch Res.

R. Severn

Afon Clywedog

Dinas Res.

River Wye

Afon Rheidol

Afon Rheidol

R. Ystwyth

Afon Elan

Craig Goch Res.

Afon Teifi

Llyn Teifi

Pen-y-garreg Res.

Afon Elan

River Wye

Carreg Ddu Res.

Llyn Gynon

Claerwen Res.

Caban-coch Res.

Llyn Berwyn

R. Camddwr

Afon Tywi

Afon Cammarch

Afon Doethie

R. Irfon

Afon Pysgotwr

Llyn Brianne Res.

Afon Tywi

Afon Cothi

Above 600

500–600

400–500

300–400

Below 300

height above sea level in metres

9

Fig 4

Landscape types

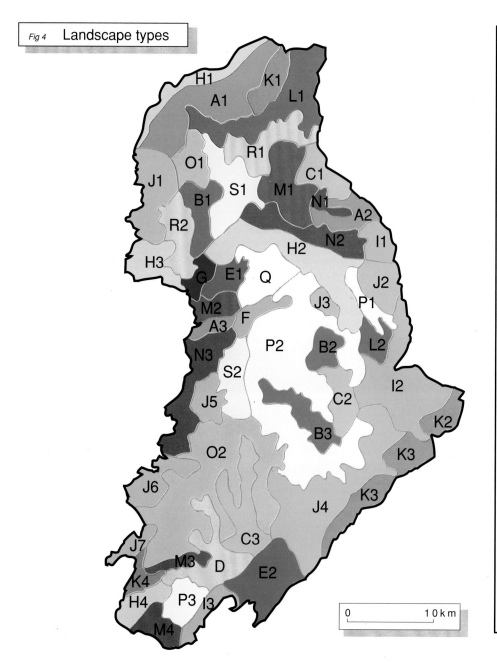

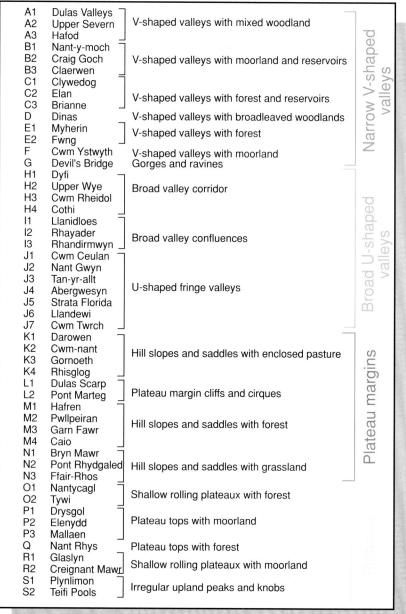

A1	Dulas Valleys	V-shaped valleys with mixed woodland	
A2	Upper Severn		
A3	Hafod		
B1	Nant-y-moch	V-shaped valleys with moorland and reservoirs	
B2	Craig Goch		
B3	Claerwen		
C1	Clywedog	V-shaped valleys with forest and reservoirs	Narrow V-shaped valleys
C2	Elan		
C3	Brianne		
D	Dinas	V-shaped valleys with broadleaved woodlands	
E1	Myherin	V-shaped valleys with forest	
E2	Fwng		
F	Cwm Ystwyth	V-shaped valleys with moorland	
G	Devil's Bridge	Gorges and ravines	
H1	Dyfi	Broad valley corridor	
H2	Upper Wye		
H3	Cwm Rheidol		
H4	Cothi		
I1	Llanidloes	Broad valley confluences	Broad U-shaped valleys
I2	Rhayader		
I3	Rhandirmwyn		
J1	Cwm Ceulan	U-shaped fringe valleys	
J2	Nant Gwyn		
J3	Tan-yr-allt		
J4	Abergwesyn		
J5	Strata Florida		
J6	Llandewi		
J7	Cwm Twrch		
K1	Darowen	Hill slopes and saddles with enclosed pasture	
K2	Cwm-nant		
K3	Gornoeth		
K4	Rhisglog		
L1	Dulas Scarp	Plateau margin cliffs and cirques	
L2	Pont Marteg		
M1	Hafren	Hill slopes and saddles with forest	Plateau margins
M2	Pwllpeiran		
M3	Garn Fawr		
M4	Caio		
N1	Bryn Mawr	Hill slopes and saddles with grassland	
N2	Pont Rhydgaled		
N3	Ffair-Rhos		
O1	Nantycagl	Shallow rolling plateaux with forest	
O2	Tywi		
P1	Drysgol	Plateau tops with moorland	
P2	Elenydd		
P3	Mallaen		
Q	Nant Rhys	Plateau tops with forest	
R1	Glaslyn	Shallow rolling plateaux with moorland	
R2	Creignant Mawr		
S1	Plynlimon	Irregular upland peaks and knobs	
S2	Teifi Pools		

0   10km

Irregular upland peaks and knobs

Landscape character

These are among the wildest and most unusual of the upland plateau landscapes. The topography is complex with rocky, eroded hills, ridges and summits rising to over 700 m. Small lakes and peat cuttings lie between the ridges. The land is covered by continuous windswept moorland, mostly *nardus* and fescue grassland, with cotton grass and other bog vegetation in the low-lying wet areas. The intricacies of landform and the differences in vegetation textures and seasonal colours give the landscape subtle variety. Views from the high points are distant and panoramic, sometimes appearing to show an unending succession of moorland and mountain ridges stretching away as far as the eye can see. There is little sign of human influence and the landscape gives a rare sense of open wildness and freedom. Large parts of these areas are common land and/or are designated as SSSIs.

Sub areas

Plynlimon has large-scale topographic variation and includes the mountain ridges of the five summits of the Plynlimon Massif. Teifi Pools is a distinct area, whose topographic variation is still marked but on a much reduced scale, being in effect a series of parallel, broken north-south ridges interspersed with a series of pools. Unless from ridge tops, views are restricted by the intricate, broken topography.

Access and recreation

Plynlimon is the well-known symbol of the Cambrian Mountains. The Teifi Pools and the Plynlimon range provide some of the most dramatic upland moorland walks in the ESA, lying on the route of the once proposed Cambrian Way and connecting into the adjacent Elenydd and Glaslyn plateaux respectively.

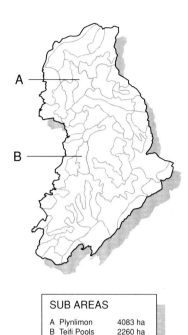

SUB AREAS

A	Plynlimon	4083 ha
B	Teifi Pools	2260 ha
	Total area	6343 ha

Key elements

Sense of elevation; unobstructed views; horizontal or rounded topography, appearing to drop away in all directions; uniform vegetation cover and fine texture of grassland; occasional features such as cairns or small lakes.

Dominant colours

Muted golden browns, yellows and greens, with dark accents of rock or peat; sky-coloured patches of water. Weather influences very important.

Descriptive terms

Exposed, wild, sparse/barren, undisturbed, continuous, uniform, horizontal, rare, muted/monochrome, threatening/unsettling, spectacular, forbidding.

Discordant elements

Intrusions which disrupt feelings of remoteness and naturalness, or interrupt the apparent continuity of open moorland.

Plateau tops with moorland

Landscape character

These plateau tops form the main upland expanses of the Cambrian Mountains. Rounded ridges of continuous moorland recede into the distance creating a sense of openness and remoteness. Elevation ranges from 450–550 m and the landscape is high, horizontal and exposed, dropping sharply to valleys at the margins. The land is covered by rough moorland grazing, varying with soil conditions and including wetter bog vegetation together with heather and bilberry on eroding peat.

Sub areas

Elenydd is the most extensive area of plateau tops, covering 170 km². The Mallaen and Drysgol tops are much smaller and lie towards the edges of the ESA where the sensations of extent and wildness, though not as great, are still significant.

Access and recreation

The attraction of this landscape type lies in its characteristic remoteness and emptiness. Apart from the mountain road from Rhayader to Cwmystwyth, across the Elenydd, the plateau tops are inaccessible to cars. They are the realm of sheep and walkers and much has been written about their value as areas of lonely wilderness typifying the 'great Welsh desert'.

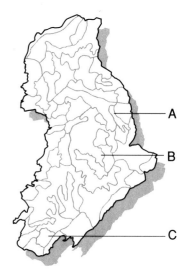

SUB AREAS		
A	Drysgol	1260 ha
B	Elenydd	16875 ha
C	Mallaen	1825 ha
Total area		19960 ha

Key elements

Windswept grass ridges and peaks, hills and small lakes; rock outcrops; continuity of vegetation; long views over open moorland.

Dominant colours

Olive greens, golden browns, russet and cream of grass moorland; darker areas of heather and bilberry; grey of rocks, water and occasional tracks; reflected light from water. Weather influences very important. Sunshine makes the grassland glow.

Descriptive terms

Uniform, exposed, wild, sparse/barren, undisturbed/balanced, horizontal, rare, muted/monochrome, threatening/unsettling, spectacular, forbidding.

Discordant elements

Any features which detract from the naturalness of the area, or which interrupt the long views of continuous moorland – notably improved grassland and forestry plantations.

Plateau tops with forest

Landscape character

Similar in landform to plateau tops with moorland, but extensive conifer plantations severely limit access and views. The open wilderness of the moorland is replaced by large expanses of afforestation with harsh geometric edges. Some areas of rough or improved grassland remain between the plantations.

Sub area

The Nant Rhys plantation is the only example of this landscape type.

Access and recreation

Much of the area is inaccessible, but a steep cul-de-sac mountain road passes alongside the forest. Bridleway and footpath routes cross the area alongside the stream channel.

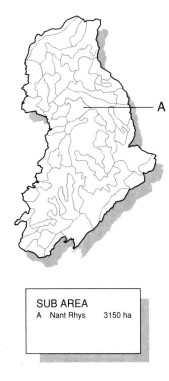

A

SUB AREA

A	Nant Rhys	3150 ha

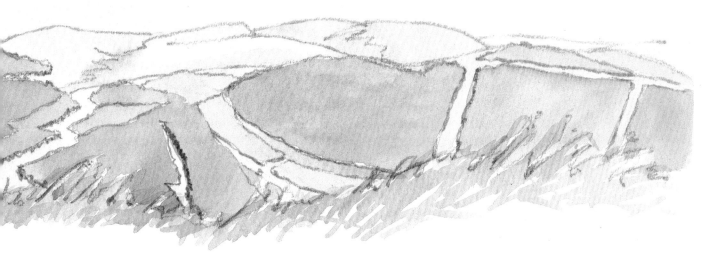

Key elements

Coniferous forest; rough or improved grassland; tracks.

Dominant colours

Dark green and glaucous conifers; grey exposed rock scars; light green/brown of remaining grassland.

Descriptive terms

Exposed, managed, disturbed, horizontal, interrupted, hostile, uninspiring.

Discordant elements

Farm tracks cutting across slopes; harsh plantation edges; felling coupes; new plantation furrows and ditches; imbalance between open and afforested land.

Shallow rolling plateaux with moorland

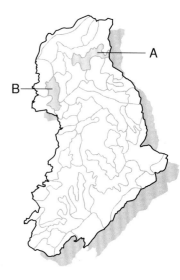

Landscape character

Plateau areas characterised by rolling, but rather indistinct, topography with a mixture of slopes, valleys and boggy depressions. Mixed moorland vegetation, with dark heather/bilberry in places, contrasts with lighter grassland areas and provides varied texture. Broad hollows are sometimes filled with small water bodies and reservoirs. Elevations range from 300–500 m. Occasional farm buildings, fences, roads, mine workings, improved pasture and distant views of forestry plantation edges are evidence of man's hand. These landscapes have some of the sense of openness found on the plateau tops, but less of the wild remoteness.

Sub areas

The Glaslyn area is characterised by substantial areas of improved land near Dylife, but also has very varied moorland vegetation with an abundance of heather and bilberry, especially around Glaslyn Lake. Creignant Mawr is predominantly rough grassland and includes the disused mine workings south of Ponterwyd.

Access and recreation

The Glaslyn plateau is crossed by the popular mountain road from Llanidloes to Machynlleth and by Glyndwr's Way long distance footpath. Several walks spread out from the Glaslyn nature reserve with good views down over the Dulas Scarp.

The Creignant Mawr plateau is crossed by the A44 trunk road and the minor roads running north and south-east from Ponterwyd. Llywernog Mining Museum lies in the area and there are interesting mining remains at Ystumtuen, and a youth hostel. Some of the lakes are used by fishing clubs.

Key elements

Broad sweeps; continuity of vegetation; small lakes; colour and contrast from heather in some locations.

Dominant colours

Golden browns, yellow, greens, dark browns, and purples of mixed moorland, subject to marked seasonal changes; contrast of bright green improved pastures; reflected colours from water surfaces.

Descriptive terms

Exposed, wild, sparse, undisturbed, continuous, horizontal, unique, accented, unsettling, scenic, remote, evocative.

Discordant elements

Improved pasture which breaks continuity of moorland vegetation; forestry plantations which break skylines.

Shallow rolling plateaux with forest

Landscape character

Similar in landform to shallow rolling plateaux with moorland, but distinguished by extensive conifer forests which cover large areas. Dark conifer plantations contrast sharply with open moorland vegetation and often dominate the landscape. In some areas, interlocking spurs of bare moorland and conifer forests combine successfully with pools and small reservoirs to create a harmonious landscape. In other areas, harsh plantation edges create discordant lines across the landscape, detracting from the rolling landform and intruding into adjacent landscape areas.

Sub areas

The Nantycagl area provides some good examples of successful relationships between afforestation, lakes and moorland, though any extensions of existing forestry could destroy this. The Tywi area has one of the most extensive areas of afforestation in the ESA. Where plantations lie in lower ground they emphasise the undulations of the landform, but forest edges on high ground intrude into neighbouring landscape types.

Access and recreation

The areas of open moorland which remain between the conifer plantations leave these plateaux reasonably penetrable to walkers and there are numerous footpaths both in open country and in the forests. The Tywi area is crossed by the once proposed Cambrian Way long distance walk and by routes linking a network of youth hostels. Activities such as walking and riding, from bases at Llanwrtyd Wells and Tregaron, also cross this area. The ridge tops offer distant views and provide good walking destinations. The Angler's Retreat Lakes, Llyn Nantycagl and Llyn Berwyn, provide focal points for visitors as well as fishing lakes. Finally, the popular scenic routes from Tal-y-bont to Nant-y-moch and from Abergwesyn to Tregaron on the old Drover's road cross through the middle of these plateaux, passing through a varied sequence of moorland and forest.

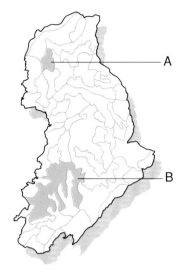

SUB AREAS

A	Nantycagl	1805 ha
B	Tywi	12978 ha
	Total area	14783 ha

Key elements

Broad sweeps of open grass moorland interlocking with large sweeps of dark forestry plantation.

Dominant colours

Golden browns, olive greens, rust and cream colours of grassland; dark green or glaucous colour of plantations.

Descriptive terms

Open/exposed, rough, continuous/interrupted, horizontal, monochrome, undistinguished/scenic, striking, interesting.

Discordant elements

Imbalance between open and afforested land; improved agricultural land; harsh plantation edges.

Plateau margin cliffs and cirques

Landscape character

This landscape type is typified by undulating lines of cliffs, steep escarpments and scree slopes, which make a sharp break between the upper plateaux and adjacent lower valleys, and often provide dramatic views from above and a strong backdrop edge to views from below. There is a general pattern of moorland sweeping down off the plateaux over smooth escarpment slopes and down to the wooded valleys and enclosed pastures below. The escarpments are accented by cliffs, rock outcrops and cirques with waterfalls. In places, improved pasture and geometric conifer plantations interrupt the smooth flow of the landform and often strike a discordant note.

Sub areas

The Dulas Scarp forms a long backdrop edge to the valleys which flow down to the Dyfi in the north. It can be seen from a long distance as a single, linear landscape feature. The Dulas Scarp also forms the western side of the Twymyn Valley where the cliffs and cirques are part of a tighter enclosure. The Pont Marteg area is a dramatic amphitheatre in the Wye Valley.

Access and recreation

The mountain road from Llanidloes to Machynlleth, designated as a scenic route, runs down over the escarpment giving panoramic views of the Dulas Scarp, especially at Craig y Maes and Foel Fadian. This is a well-used tourist route. Glaslyn is a popular area for walking and a number of paths, including Glyndwr's Way, skirt along the crest of the escarpment before dropping down towards the Dyfi Valley. The cliffs and cirques at Pont Marteg provide a particularly dramatic landscape on the A470 trunk road, north of Rhayader, and may be seen by many visitors as the gateway to the Cambrian Mountains. The minor road through the area provides popular parking and picnicking spots.

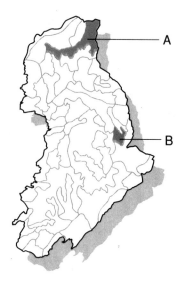

SUB AREAS
A Dulas Scarp   5290 ha
B Pont Marteg   1260 ha
Total area   6550 ha

Key elements

Cliffs/escarpments; smooth scree slides and waterfalls; circular shape of some bowls; differentiation of moorland on plateaux and farmland below; long views from edge of escarpment.

Dominant colours

Strong contrast of greens of pasture land below with dark browns, greys and purples from exposed rock, bracken and heather of escarpment.

Descriptive terms

Open, domestic/wild, lush, balanced, complex, harmonious, stepped, unique, colourful, comfortable/unsettling, spectacular, welcoming/forbidding.

Discordant elements

Forestry plantations which interrupt the flow of the landform and obscure outward views; intrusions into the setting of waterfalls and gorges; agricultural reclamation which breaks the pattern of moorland above and pasture below; roads which cut zigzags up steep slopes.

Hill slopes and saddles with grassland

Landscape character

A transitional landscape type representing a gradual change from the plateau moorlands to the lower valleys. Hill slopes and saddles with grassland usually occur at higher elevations (300-500 m) and the land cover reflects the more hostile climate. The hill slopes tend to be covered with rough grazing, and the hollows and boggy ground with rushes. These landscapes can be wild, open extensions of descending moorland but in places they are fragmented, desolate areas of wire fences, improved grassland and small, incongruous blocks of conifer shelterbelts or farm plantations, all creating a rather discordant landscape.

Sub areas

Bryn Mawr and Pont Rhydgaled are long narrow areas on the edge of the Hafren Forest and are characterised by improved grassland, wire fences and shelterbelts. The Ffair-Rhos area, on the western edge of the ESA, is more extensive, with areas of rough grassland and bracken.

Access and recreation

These areas generally tend to be away from main access routes, although they may sometimes be crossed when travelling from one part of the Cambrian Mountains to another. The Ffair-Rhos area has the north–south route via the B4343 at its western edge. There are numerous footpaths in all these areas. Ceredigion District Council's suggested inland footpath route passes through the Ffair-Rhos area between Hafod and Strata Florida.

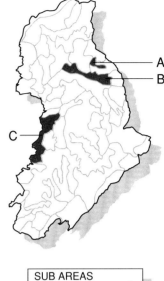

SUB AREAS	
A Bryn Mawr	600 ha
B Pont Rhydgaled	3145 ha
C Ffair-Rhos	4045 ha
Total area	7790 ha

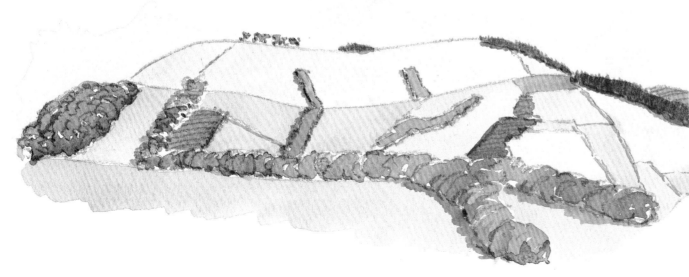

Key elements

Lack of abrupt changes in topography or land cover; gradual transitions from upland to lowland; views over lowland.

Dominant colours

Bright green of pasture land; darker greens/browns of hedges, hedgerows and woodlands; dull olive/yellow green of upland rough grazing; seasonal russet of bracken slopes; grey of rock and roads.

Descriptive terms

Open, rough, sparse, managed, disturbed, uniform, balanced/discordant, layered, unsettling, muted.

Discordant elements

Sharp breaks and boundaries in land cover; scars from road cuttings across gentle slopes; improved grassland; wire fences; conifer shelterbelt blocks.

Hill slopes and saddles with forest

Landscape character

Topographically similar to the previous type and again lying at higher elevations (300–500 m) directly on the edges of upland plateaux. Distinguished from the other hill slopes and saddles areas by the presence of large-scale forestry plantations across the majority of the slopes. Views are generally restricted, although openings occur where clear felling has taken place. Forestry edges are often planted up to ownership boundaries and finish in harsh vertical lines across hillsides which can be seen from some distance.

Sub areas

Hafren is extensively afforested. Caio has large areas of forestry plantations mixed with tongues of rough grazing and inbye land that give a more varied landscape. In Pwllpeiran and Garn Fawr less than half of the area is afforested, creating open spaces between plantations but often revealing harsh forest edges.

Access and recreation

The Hafren Forest incorporates popular picnic sites and forest walks but many parts of these forests are thick, dark and often impenetrable. Detailed attention to design at the time of second rotation could make these areas much more attractive to visitors and walkers.

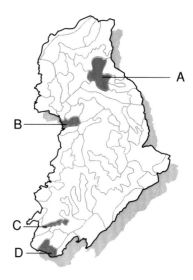

SUB AREAS	
A Hafren	4095 ha
B Pwllpeiran	1383 ha
C Garn Fawr	720 ha
D Caio	1833 ha
Total Area	9031 ha

Key elements

Coniferous forest; improved grassland.

Dominant colours

Dark green of plantations; brown/grey of rocks, soil and roads; lighter colours of larch.

Descriptive terms

Closed, managed, ragged/trim, disturbed, interrupted/continuous, discordant/balanced, unusual, monochrome/muted, dangerous, unpleasant/scenic, unexpected.

Discordant elements

Straight forestry tracks and firebreaks; felling coupes; harsh plantation edges.

Hill slopes and saddles with enclosed pasture

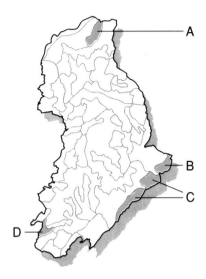

Landscape character

Similar landform to the other hill slopes and saddles types but generally lying below an elevation of 300 m. Short stream valleys segment the areas into a series of hills and saddles with gentle slopes. At the lower elevations these landscapes are generally covered by bosky farmland with lush pastures, enclosed by hedges and hedgerow trees. Broadleaved woodlands nestle within this framework, connecting to riparian vegetation or forming low, wooded caps to the domed hilltops. Farm buildings and villages are scattered through these areas.

Sub areas

Darowen and Rhisglog are small sheltered farmland areas, whereas Cwm-nant and Gornoeth form an extensive area on the south-eastern edge of the ESA, backed by the broader and wilder U-shaped fringe valleys of Abergwesyn.

Access and recreation

These are essentially farmed landscapes which, rather than offering specific attractions for visitors, provide attractive countryside to tour through, or sometimes to stay in.

Key elements

Undulating landform; enclosed pastures; bosky woodland; thick hedgerows; small farmsteads.

Dominant colours

Bright green pasture; greens and browns of deciduous woodland; white and red accents from farm houses.

Descriptive terms

Varied, harmonious, calm, lush, managed, comfortable, interesting, pleasant.

Discordant elements

Conifer blocks; hedgerow removal.

Gorges and ravines

Landscape character

Steep and rocky incised river gorges with sheer cliffs, rapids and waterfalls. Valley sides rise steeply by up to 150 m and are covered in thick, semi-natural oak woodland. Bare and rocky rough moorland ridges contrast strongly with dense wooded valley sides. Views of the gorges from the surrounding area often come as a surprise and make a strong impact.

Sub area

The Rheidol gorge system at Devil's Bridge is the only example of this landscape type.

Access and recreation

Devil's Bridge is one of the best known visitor attractions in the Cambrian Mountains, with up to 200,000 visitors a year. The wooded gorges are a major part of the attraction of the area.

SUB AREA

A Devil's Bridge 1070 ha

Key elements

Dramatic cliffs and waterfalls; natural appearance of woods and rock formations; strong contrast with surrounding areas; feelings of remoteness and isolation in the gorges.

Dominant colours

Contrasting dark rock and white water; dark greens of woods; russet/greys of bracken and cliffs; accentuated by extremes of light and shadow. Colour accents from signs and tourist shops, phone boxes, dams and related structures.

Descriptive terms

Confined, rough/wild, lush, undisturbed, diverse, vertical, unique, colourful, threatening, spectacular, foreign, forbidding.

Discordant elements

Features which interrupt the feelings of naturalness and remoteness that characterise these landscapes, including facilities for visitors in the gorges themselves and forestry plantations in place of deciduous woodlands.

V-shaped valleys with moorland

Landscape character

These valleys are steep-sided and angular with very little improved valley land. The stream or river channel dominates the valley bottom and is sometimes marked by a border of shrubs and trees. Often there is a terraced road line on the valley side, with wider terraces for lay-bys or junctions. There is generally less differentiation or pattern in land cover than in the broad and U-shaped valleys.

Sub area

Cwm Ystwyth is the only example of this landform type which is not afforested or filled by a reservoir and inbye land, and is hence a unique landscape type. It is a bleak upland valley with rough moorland grass vegetation cladding the steep, angular sides. There is very little improved land and the prominent features are bare scree, waste tips and the abandoned buildings of old lead mines. Glacial features such as moraines give added interest to the landscape.

Access and recreation

With its bleak character and abandoned lead mines, Cwm Ystwyth is a unique valley. It forms part of the popular scenic moorland drive from Rhayader to Hafod and Pont-rhyd-y-groes. This is an ancient route which now provides a rare opportunity for car-borne visitors to cross the high moorlands. The lead mines are of interest to some visitors.

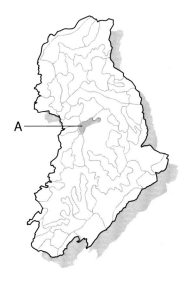

SUB AREA	
A Cwm Ystwyth	1355 ha

Key elements

Bare, rough grassland; sharp edge at horizon; tightly framed corridor views; remains of lead mining; river channel.

Dominant colours

Dull olive green of valley sides; grey of road, mine workings and rock outcrops.

Descriptive terms

Exposed, rough, barren, derelict, interrupted, discordant, stepped, rare, threatening, spectacular, monochrome, forbidding.

Discordant elements

Small farm conifer blocks; improved grassland; alterations to stream channel; cut and fill for roads on bare valley sides.

V-shaped valleys with moorland and reservoirs

Landscape character

The topography is similar to V-shaped valleys with moorland, but the valley floor and lower slopes are occupied by reservoirs. The water surface, with its drawdown zone, is the dominant element. Gently sloping valley sides, with some scree slopes and rocky outcrops, sweep down to the water. Land cover is upland rough grazing, consisting almost entirely of moorland grasses with some patches of bracken. Dams and associated structures and trees are features in the landscape. Roads form scars around the reservoirs.

Sub areas

The Nant-y-moch Reservoir lies in the forked upland valley head of the Afon Rheidol. To the east of the reservoir, rough grass moorland rises steeply into the Plynlimon Massif but, to the west, conifer plantations intrude on the moorland. The Craig Goch and Claerwen Reservoirs are long, narrow water bodies in the Elan Valley. They are completely surrounded by grass moorland.

Access and recreation

The moorland reservoirs of Claerwen, Craig Goch and Nant-y-moch are popular destinations for visitors, both to drive around and as a base from which to walk. The open character of the land provides long and panoramic views for walkers, and contrasts with the forested valleys and reservoirs lower down.

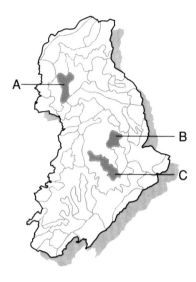

SUB AREAS		
A Nant-y-moch	2130 ha
B Craig Goch	1330 ha
C Claerwen	2510 ha
Total area	5970 ha

Key elements

Reflective water surface of reservoir; drawdown zone; rough grazing; dams and associated structures.

Dominant colours

Grey of water; olive/yellow green of grassland; russet of bracken; grey of roads, dams, scree slopes and rocks; accents of dark green from trees near dams.

Descriptive terms

Open/exposed, rough, barren, balanced/tended, continuous, horizontal, unusual, muted/monochrome.

Discordant elements

Road cuttings; wire fences; forestry plantations.

V-shaped valleys with forest

Landscape character

Landform characteristics similar to V-shaped valleys with moorland but differentiated by being largely covered with continuous, coniferous plantations which sweep over large parts of each area. Characteristically, forestry runs unbroken over ridge lines and right down to the river edge. Views and access are limited by forestry, even along the valley bottoms. Forest boundaries, which are largely determined by ownership rather than landform, often create harsh lines across the landscape and intrude into neighbouring landscape zones.

Sub areas

The Myherin area is almost completely afforested but the Fwng area still retains grassland ridges within the forest.

Access and recreation

Large sections of these areas are owned by the Forestry Commission. They are not traversed by public roads but walking is permitted on footpaths and forestry tracks, although views from these routes are limited and there is often little incentive to venture far into the forest. The Myherin Forest lies close to the B4574 route which links the Cwm Ystwyth road and Devil's Bridge. The Fwng area is partly overlooked by the Sugar Loaf vista point and the Heart of Wales railway line passes through the area for about 3 miles.

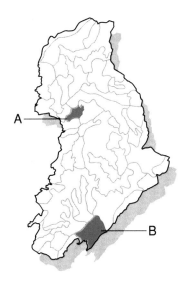

SUB AREAS	
A Myherin	1335 ha
B Fwng	4355 ha
Total area	5690 ha

Key elements

Conifer plantations; rocky streams; patches of improved grassland; forestry fencing; felling coupes.

Dominant colours

Dark green and glaucous conifers; seasonal light green and yellow of larch; grey/brown of brash and felling coupes; pale green of improved grassland.

Descriptive terms

Closed, managed, disturbed, continuous, stepped, monochrome, threatening, remote, striking.

Discordant elements

Harsh plantation or felling coupe edges; conifer plantations crowding stream edges.

V-shaped valleys with forest and reservoirs

Landscape character

Landform characteristics again similar to the other V-shaped valleys but differentiated by being flooded to form reservoirs and by the associated mixed forestry and amenity planting. Forested or wooded spurs, bare grassland promontories and water often interlock to form a distinctive and attractive landscape.

Sub areas

The interleaving of bare promontories and well designed forested spurs is particularly evident at Llyn Brianne. The upper Tywi and Camddwr valleys, which lead down into Llyn Brianne, are rather different from the other areas. The valleys are narrower and the reservoir only becomes visible gradually as one progresses from north to south. The bare western flank of the Camddwr Valley and the partially bare eastern flank of the upper Tywi Valley create interesting landscape contrasts. The Elan Valley reservoirs are distinguished by valley-side broadleaved woodlands, steep rocky heather-clad slopes and distinctive Victorian engineering structures, while Llyn Clywedog is rather more open.

Access and recreation

All these reservoirs are major visitor attractions providing popular scenic routes around the edges and stopping places at various vista points and picnic sites. There are short walks and trails available at each reservoir and the Elan Valley Visitor Centre is an important attraction. Water sports take place at Llyn Clywedog.

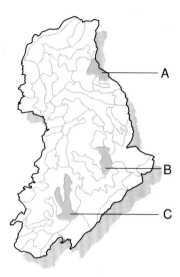

SUB AREAS	
A Clywedog	1662 ha
B Elan	1938 ha
C Brianne	3468 ha
Total area	7068 ha

Key elements

Continuous steep slope of valley sides; sharp horizon often formed by forestry plantation spreading up from valley and over ridgeline; water in reservoir valley; forestry.

Dominant colours

Dark green of forestry plantations, sometimes with mixed greens from variation in species; dark grey/brown of rock outcrops and stream course; dull olive green of rough grassland; light reflected contrasts from reservoirs and streams; seasonal accents of russet bracken, red rowan and yellow larch.

Descriptive terms

Closed, rough, managed, balanced, diverse, stepped, accented, scenic/picturesque, accessible, active.

Discordant elements

Cut and fill for roads on valley sides; large-scale felling coupes; drawdown on the reservoir edges and especially in the shallow upper arms.

V-shaped valleys with mixed woodland

Landscape character

Landform similar to previous V-shaped valleys but distinguished by land use and land cover. These valleys retain areas of broadleaved woodland but large sections of the valley sides have been cleared as pasture or for coniferous plantations. The valley floors are narrow but lush and inbye pastures flank the rivers and sometimes spread up the lower valley slopes. Hedgerows and riverside trees enclose the valley bottom inbye land. Bare moorland ridge tops are often visible above the mid-slope woodland.

Sub areas

The Dulas Valleys in the north tend to be shorter and more intimate than those in the Upper Severn area, namely the Severn, Clywedog and Ystwyth Valleys. In the Hafod area, the lower Ystwyth Valley is a special case because of the Hafod Estate and the remnants of Thomas Johnes' historic landscape.

Access and recreation

The scenic Llyfnant and Artists' Valleys in the north-west are well-known beauty spots, although they are off the beaten track. The other northern valleys also provide popular scenic routes, especially the Dulas Valley, as do the Severn and Clywedog Valleys. The Hafod Valley is skirted by the B4764 road to Pont-rhyd-y-groes. All these areas include numerous footpaths and tracks and often contain tourist accommodation.

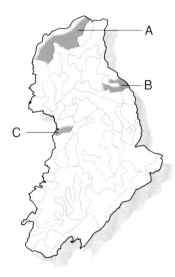

SUB AREAS		
A	Dulas Valleys	6405 ha
B	Upper Severn	1683 ha
C	Hafod	715 ha
	Total area	8803 ha

Key elements

Shelter provided by close, steep valley sides; forest and woodland interspersed with rough grassland, bracken and rocks; well-tended, improved pasture land.

Dominant colours

Greens of deciduous trees; muted grey colours of brash, tree trunks, rock outcrops and water; browns, russets, and olive green of rough moorland and grassland with bracken; bright green of improved pasture; seasonal variations in trees and moorland.

Descriptive terms

Sheltered/confined, wild, lush, diverse, harmonious, colourful, safe, scenic, evocative.

Discordant elements

Cut and fill for roads on valley sides; electricity lines; harsh plantation edges and top margins.

V-shaped valleys with broadleaved woodlands

Landscape character

These valleys are similar in form to the other V-shaped valleys, though they tend to be narrower, steeper and craggier. They are distinguished by being extensively and almost exclusively covered by semi-natural, broadleaved woodland, or rough grassland and bracken. Small areas of inbye land are maintained on the valley floor.

Sub areas

The only examples of these valleys are in the Dinas area and they represent a unique remnant of the historic valley landscapes of the Cambrian Mountains. The area includes the upland heads of the valleys which are shallower and less rugged and are more likely to include improved pasture.

Access and recreation

These valleys are particularly popular with bird watchers who visit the RSPB's Dinas reserve. The area is a well-known visitor destination and part of an SSSI which stretches up into the plateaux to the north and south and is famous for its birds of prey. The scenic road to Llyn Brianne and the road through the Cothi Valley both pass through the area. A number of popular walks exist, including the route to the youth hostel at Tyn-y-cornel.

SUB AREA	
A Dinas	4185 ha

Key elements

Oak woodland; lush inbye pasture on valley floor; rock outcrops, bracken and rough moorland on upper valley sides; narrow rocky streams and waterfalls.

Dominant colours

Rich, dark greens and browns of oak woodland; pale olive greens and russets of rough grass and bracken; lush green of inbye pasture; glint of stream water in sunlight; seasonal variations in woodland and moorland.

Descriptive terms

Sheltered, wild, lush, undisturbed, diverse, harmonious, vertical, rare, accented.

Discordant elements

Coniferous planting; intrusion of adjacent afforestation onto surrounding skylines.

U-shaped fringe valleys

Landscape character

Valleys with a distinctive U-shape, generally occurring on the fringes of the ESA. Similar in landform to broad valley corridors but lying in the upstream section of rivers on plateau edges. Generally straight valleys up to 4 km long with a smooth flat bottom of 200–500 m wide, enclosed by valley sides rising steeply by 150 m or more. These valleys form the largest single landscape type in the ESA and although they are all similar in form, they vary considerably in land cover. Typically, U-shaped valleys are bleak and open with riverside trees and inbye land on the valley floor, giving way to dry grassland, bracken and rocks on the valley sides. The valley heads typically form distinctive moorland bowls rising up to the plateau edge, although sometimes these bowls are now covered by substantially improved grassland. In some cases broadleaved woodland remains on the lower and middle valley slopes. In many cases, however, conifers have been planted over the valley head bowls or in blocks along the valley sides. These plantations tend to be harsh geometric shapes, often detracting from the valley form and running up over ridge lines, intruding into adjacent plateau areas.

Sub areas

The number of U-shaped valleys and their occurrence all round the fringes of the area result in a wide variety of individual landscapes. For example, the bare and craggy Abergwesyn and Llandewi valleys contrast with the gentler wooded Tan-yr-allt valleys. The bare moorland Cwm Ceulan valley head contrasts with the forested Strata Florida head. Each valley has its own particular character and combination of features.

Access and recreation

Public access and provision for recreation varies widely in these valleys. A number contain well-known scenic roads, for example the Abergwesyn/Tregaron drover's road passes through the Abergwesyn, Cwm Irfon and Tregaron valleys, and the Nant-y-Moch/Tal-y-bont route through Cwm Ceulan. Others are less well used but still valued by local people. Many footpaths are present and some of the rough, open valleys, for example the Afon Gwesyn, provide useful routes onto the high plateaux. The valleys around Abergwesyn and Llanwrtyd Wells are particularly well used and contain a number of accommodation bases.

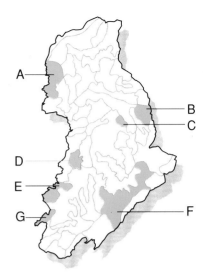

SUB AREAS		
A	Cwm Ceulan	3950 ha
B	Nant Gwyn	1998 ha
C	Tan-yr-allt	810 ha
D	Strata Florida	1568 ha
E	Llandewi	2290 ha
F	Abergwesyn	9098 ha
G	Cwm Twrch	925 ha
Total area		20639 ha

Key elements

U-shaped valley form; diversity of elements and variety in landscape; intimate agricultural landscape in enclosed inbye areas; steep valley sides with rough grazing; woodland and forestry plantations; sweeps of rough grazing across parts of the valley.

Dominant colours

Olive greens, yellow-browns of valley side rough grazing, dark greens of woods and forestry plantations on valley sides, bright greens of inbye land, seasonal colour accents of russet bracken on valley sides and red from rowan trees, grey of rock outcrops.

Descriptive terms

Closed, managed, diverse, stepped, unusual, colourful, safe, scenic, striking, approachable, static, evocative.

Discordant elements

Forestry plantations on the plateau which break the skylines or creep down into the valleys; land cover boundaries forming marked vertical lines; decline in standard of management of inbye land.

Broad valley corridor

Landscape character

Wide, downstream river corridors with flat valley bottoms and high, enclosing valley sides. The valley floors are usually characterised by lush pasture and hedgerows with occasional clumps of riparian trees along the river. The valley sides rise between 150–200 m with broad sweeps of forest or woodland along the mid-slopes, alternating with improved grassland and bracken. The upper flanks and shoulders become more barren and severe with open rough grazing, bracken and rock scarps and bare open moorland ridgelines.

Sub areas

The Dyfi, Cwm Rheidol and Cothi Valleys all have generous sweeps, with broadleaved and mixed woodland on the valley slopes above wide meandering rivers. The Upper Wye Valley, by contrast, lies at a higher elevation, with steep valley sides and extensive conifer plantations interspersed with rough moorland.

Access and recreation

Road corridors extend down each of the broad valleys providing some of the main views of the area to passing traffic. The views from lay-bys and vista points, as well as the slopes on the opposite side of the valley to the road, are visible to large numbers of travellers. The Cothi Valley contains the National Trust's Dolaucothi Gold Mines, an important visitor attraction in the area. The Rheidol area includes the Rheidol Valley Railway and the Forestry Commission's Rheidol Visitor Centre. The Upper Wye Valley provides the corridor for the main east-west route through the Cambrian Mountains, the A44 trunk road.

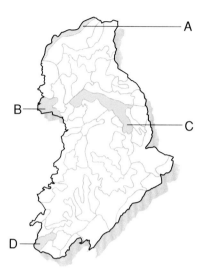

SUB AREAS		
A	Dyfi	1805 ha
B	Cwm Rheidol	2173 ha
C	Upper Wye	5878 ha
D	Cothi	1510 ha
	Total area	11366 ha

Key elements

Broad meandering river, lush pastures, hedgerows, riparian trees and farm settlements on valley floor; mixed woodland or plantations and improved grassland on valley sides; rocks and rough moorland on ridge tops.

Dominant colours

Lush greens of pasture; white and red accents of farm settlements; dark greens of mixed woodland and forestry; water reflecting light; olive greens, russets and greys of moorland; seasonal changes in deciduous woodland and moorland grasses.

Descriptive terms

Tended, lush, diverse, layered, picturesque, accessible.

Discordant elements

Cut and fill scars from road construction; cluttered lay-bys; mining scars; harsh forestry plantation and felling coupe edges.

Broad valley confluences

Landscape character

Wide valleys of up to 4 km across at the base, often where several tributary valleys converge. Valley sides rise between 150–200 m. Similar to broad valley corridors, but the width of the confluences reduces the sense of geographic enclosure. Valley floors and lower flanks are characterised by lush pasture, hedgerow trees and occasional small, round hills. Small market towns lie at road junctions, and clusters of farm buildings are scattered over the valley floor and lower sides. In places, poorer, boggy ground lies fallow or has been planted with small conifer blocks. Middle valley slopes often covered by extensive plantations and marked by geometric shapes of improved pasture, forest edges, road cuttings or mining scars. Upper slopes and ridge tops often remain as bare moorland, but in places plantations and improved grassland run up over the ridge in harsh contrast to the horizontal grain of the valley. Internal views within the valley confluences are limited by plantings to glimpses of distant valley ridges; but ridge-top views provide broad panoramas.

Sub areas

The Rhandirmwyn area is a notably attractive example of a broad, very bosky valley confluence. The Rhayader area is characterised by stone walls, deciduous woodlands and steep, bracken-covered slopes.

Access and recreation

The broad valley confluences lie on the eastern and southern edges of the ESA and act as entrance points to the area. Towns such as Rhayader and Llanidloes provide important tourist facilities and information points. Views of bare moorland ridges further into the area announce the Cambrian Mountains beyond. Rhandirmwyn provides the main entry point from the south to the Tywi and Cothi Valleys.

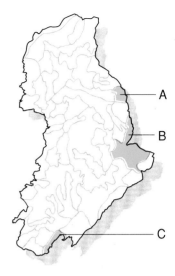

SUB AREAS	
A Llanidloes	1128 ha
B Rhayader	6330 ha
C Rhandirmwyn	1255 ha
Total area	8713 ha

Key elements

Conspicuous vertical stratification of land cover; strong agricultural pattern; bosky hedgerows, woodland blocks and distinct river courses.

Dominant colours

Bright greens of inbye land with white and red accents from some farm buildings and houses; mid-greens and autumn colours of hedgerows and deciduous woodland; dark greens of coniferous plantations; dark greys and brown of ridge and rock outcrops; russet of bracken; occasional reflected colour from water surfaces.

Descriptive terms

Lush, diverse, tended, domestic, stepped, colourful, picturesque, harmonious, familiar, welcoming, active, evocative.

Discordant elements

Poorly-managed farmland which breaks the valley bottom pattern; scarring by roads or other disturbance of valley sides; distinct land cover boundaries running vertically across the horizontal pattern; isolated patches of geometric forestry plantations or improved moorland.

3. Illustrations of landscape types

Irregular upland peaks and knobs

Shallow rolling plateaux with moorland

Plateau tops with moorland

Plateau tops with forest

Shallow rolling plateaux with forest

Plateau margin cliffs and cirques

Hill slopes and saddles with grassland

Hill slopes and saddles with forest

Gorges and ravines

Hill slopes and saddles with enclosed pasture

V-shaped valleys with moorland

V-shaped valleys with moorland and reservoirs

V-shaped valleys with forest

V-shaped valleys with forest and reservoirs

V-shaped valleys with mixed woodland

V-shaped valleys with broadleaved woodlands

U-shaped fringe valleys

Broad valley corridor

Broad valley confluences

4. Perceptions of the landscape

So far, this assessment has been concerned with the relatively objective process of understanding, describing and classifying the landscape of the Cambrian Mountains. It is important, however, to complete the picture by examining subjective reactions to the area. The way in which the landscape is perceived and valued adds a significant extra dimension.

Historic records, paintings and general descriptions of the area provide us with an insight into the way in which the Cambrian Mountains have been perceived in the past, while recent writings, artists' impressions and surveys of those currently using the area give an indication of attitudes to the ESA today.

Perceptions over the years

A considerable amount has been written about the landscape of the Cambrian Mountains over the years. The earliest records are the comments of the medieval chronicler, Giraldus Cambrensis, in 1188, and the writings of John Leland, the King's Antiquary, in 1553. Later written sources include eighteenth and nineteenth century discourses on particular areas, technical reports by those with a special concern for landscape, and today's popular guidebooks and tourist literature. The area also received particular attention in the eighteenth century because the Hafod estate of Thomas Johnes, who landscaped his grounds in the pursuit of the picturesque, became a favourite port of call for writers and painters who were touring Wales.

Historic written descriptions have tended, in general, to focus on three main types of landscapes in the area: the open upland plateaux, the more intimate wooded valleys, and the dramatic waterfalls and gorges. More recent descriptions also comment on new features in the landscape, notably reservoirs and forestry plantations. The juxtaposition and contrast between these four main landscape types combine to create the rich character of the Cambrian Mountains, and the contrasts in themselves have stimulated further observations.

The upland plateaux at the remote heart of the Cambrian Mountains seem to be regarded by many writers as the epitome of this central part of Wales, and yet this type of landscape, perhaps more than any other, shows the way in which attitudes and perceptions change with time. In 1553 John Leland described the Teifi Pools as 'horrible with the sight of bare stonies' and nearly two centuries later Daniel Defoe expressed equal antipathy to the 'barbarous' hills, dismissing the plateaux as 'a kind of desert, scarce habitable or passable' (1). In 1776 another travel writer, Thomas Pennant, condemned the area in similar terms as a 'dreary and almost uninhabited country' (2). Gilpin, too, pursuing his picturesque ideas, was not impressed, on the basis that there was 'an insufficiency of water to balance the land'. The uplands appeared inhospitable, unproductive and devoid of any aesthetic appeal – a wasteland.

It was not until the late eighteenth and early nineteenth centuries that a taste for the 'sublime' in landscape scenery began to emerge. Wales in general, and its more spectacular mountain scenery in particular, gradually begin to find favour. George Borrow, the author of *Wild Wales*, was especially struck by the dramatic gorges of the Cambrian Mountains and their contrast with the intimate wooded valleys.

"...on entering these mountains, like the prelude to some enchantment, we are presented with a contrast that is really awful, our winding road hanging on the precipitous sides of steep, smooth, and mighty hills, clothed to their very tops with verdure, bespotted all over with numerous flocks, and herds of black cattle..."

G. Cumberland, *An attempt to describe Hafod*, 1796

"...wild scenery and elegant ornament, a foaming river and rugged rocks, perpendicular precipices and lofty mountains, contrasted with rich meadows and neat enclosures, leave apparently nothing deficient to complete this singular and picturesque scene."

Jonathan Williams, *A General History of the County of Radnorshire*, 1905

"Of all the pooles none standeth in so rocky and stony soile as Tyve doth, that hath within hym many stonies. The ground all about Tyve and a great mile towards Stratfler is horrible with the sight of bare stonies."

John Leland, 1553

"...the names of some of these hills seemed as barbarous to us, who speak no Welch, as the hills themselves."

Daniel Defoe, *A Tour through the Whole Island of Great Britain: Letter 6 – The West and Wales*, 1724–26

"A mountainous wilderness extended on every side, a waste of russet-coloured hills, with here and there a black, craggy summit. No signs of life or cultivation were to be discovered, and the eye might search in vain for a grove or even a single tree."

George Borrow, *Wild Wales*, 1862

Nevertheless, Borrow's particular interest lay in the people and culture of Wales and he was disappointed by the lack of both in the Plynlimon area, describing it as 'a waste of russet-coloured hills' (3).

It is only since the Second World War and the growth of the national parks movement that the taste for wild upland scenery, and for walking in remote moorland and mountain areas, has generated widespread interest in the form of descriptions and guide books. In recent years the wildness and remoteness of the high moorlands has been increasingly treasured. In 1910 Bradley wrote of 'a glorious solitude' (4) and *The Shell Guide to Wales*, 1969 describes 'remote beauty' and 'lovely, treeless, wild country' (5). The more congested and frantic life becomes, the more the opportunity for empty solitude is relished. Fishlock writes of 'the sensation of timelessness and remoteness' (6) and Sale savours experiencing 'an isolation which does not exist to the same intensity elsewhere' (7). The degree to which attitudes have changed can be illustrated by the contrasting descriptions of the Teifi Pools; John Leland condemning the area as a bare wasteland in 1553, and Richard Sale describing it as 'some of the loveliest country of the Elenydd' (7) in 1983. Kyffin Williams, the well-known contemporary Welsh artist, has painted the Teifi Pools. He comments that he is particularly attracted by the 'whaleback ridges' and the smoothness of the whole moorland plateau. The wide open landscape provides a vast proportion of sky to land and offers impressive effects of light and cloud.

Many contemporary writers now refer wryly to the unidentified traveller who described the moors as 'a sodden weariness' and the claim of the area to be the 'great Welsh desert'. Indeed, Porter describes the Elenydd as 300 miles of 'uncompromising wilderness' (8), with which he suggests only the Scottish Highlands can vie for wildness. One of the most succinct summaries of current attitudes to the upland plateaux of the Cambrian Mountains is provided by Margaret Davies's description when the area was proposed as a national park: 'This proposed Park is the quintessence of the remote, beautiful and emptying heart of Wales – a countryside of great open moorlands'.

The wooded river valleys have not been subject to the same fluctuations in taste as the moorland plateaux. They have always been highly valued. Richard Sale suggests that drovers of old may even have chosen the road along the Doethie Valley for its aesthetic appeal. There appear to be four components which make these valleys so attractive. First, there is the shelter and enclosure of the landform. Place names, such as Pisgah (the place where Moses arrived at the edge of the wilderness and looked down over the Promised Land) give an indication of the relief and comfort offered by the valleys after the open moors. Guide books use phrases such as 'tucked away in a side valley' (5) to describe Caio.

The second component is the river at the bottom of the valley. The valley of the Afon Annell is noted for the 'mountain stream (which) comes tumbling through the trees' (5) and the broader Teifi river is described as 'wonderfully peaceful' (7). Borrow was especially moved by the Ystwyth. The third component is the lushness which sometimes characterises the valley bottom, and its ability to support better quality pasture. Bucolic valleys of rich pastures and hedgerow trees are identified with an ideal of the picturesque painted by artists such as John Cotman and Thomas Rowlandson. Finally, there is the deciduous woodland which is usually associated with these valleys. Borrow referred to the 'beautiful wooded dingles' and Shelley praised the 'valleys clothed with woods' at Cwm Elan.

"No man, no tourist, at any rate, ever penetrates these hills. For this is the great mountain wilderness ... A glorious solitude..."

A.G. Bradley, *Mid-Wales Guide Book*, 1910

"...this view (from Drygarn) will give the walker a true impression of the Elenith as it really is, vast and lifeless, with blank khaki ridges stretching as far as the eye can see."

T. Porter, 'Elenith'

"Here is a kind of loneliness and a natural hostility that I can recommend if you feel like being put in your place."

T. Fishlock, *Wales and the Welsh*, 1972

"...the lover of scenic beauty can hardly improve on the valleys of Gwenffrwd, Psygotwr and Doethie."

Richard Sale, *A Cambrian Way*, 1983

"The scenery was exceedingly beautiful. Below me was a bright green valley, at the bottom of which the Ystwyth ran brawling, now hid amongst groves, now showing a long stretch of water."

George Borrow, *Wild Wales*, 1862

"...nor is there another parish in this country, or perhaps in the Principality itself, that can exhibit more romantic scenes of Nature than those well wooded, watered and rocky yet fertile districts.."

J. Williams, *A General History of the County of Radnorshire*, 1905

To some a 'sodden weariness' to others a 'glorious solitude', the remote, empty moorland at the heart of the Cambrian Mountains has often been called the great Welsh desert.

Valleys, reservoirs and dramatic features such as the Devil's Bridge gorges all provide attractions for visitors to the area.

Teifi Pools, Kyffin Williams, (Collection of Ian Mayes).

Contemporary writers equally value the woodland. Condry wrote of the woods in the deep valleys of the Llyfnant, Einion, Clettrwr and Leri: 'these woods are so picturesque, so absolutely right' (9).

The valley landscapes appear to produce emotions of romance and enchantment in writers. They represent a fantasy landscape, inspired by a mixture of dramatic and bucolic elements. The wooded valleys are gentle, human-scale landscapes, conveying an impression of friendliness and comfort.

Waterfalls and gorges are the landscapes most often described as 'dramatic' in the Cambrian Mountains. The paintings of Richard Wilson (1713–82) are a good example of the appreciation of these spectacular landscape features of Wales. Waterfalls have attracted visitors since the eighteenth century and the falls at Devil's Bridge are still one of the most popular tourist attractions in the area. Early descriptions of the gorges and falls use a variety of emotional adjectives, such as 'noble' (Pennant), 'picturesque' (Shelley), 'breathtaking' (Belloc), and 'grand, tremendous, sublime' (1816 *Aberystwyth Guide*).

Today, visitors to Devil's Bridge may be more struck by the impact of commercial tourism than by the awe and horror which filled Borrow. Richard Sale describes the sad effects of wire fences and turnstiles; though he does admit that 'there is much here that is truly delightful' (7). In his description of the route of Glyndwr's Way, Sale also describes falls and gorges on the escarpment north of Plynlimon. He describes 'the impressive view' formed by the steep slopes of scree and hard sandstone horseshoe and waterfalls of Ffrwd Fawr as the 'impressive sweep of the rock amphitheatre over which the water hurls itself', and as the 'tremendous gorge of the upper Afon Dulas'. Margaret Davies, describing the proposed national park, also draws attention to the way the great open moorlands are 'deeply cut by splendid gorges', mentioning particularly the Llyfnant, Dulas and Twymyn gorges running north and, in the south, the 'lovely gorges' cut by the headstreams of the Tywi (10).

Reservoirs and forests are relatively new features in the Cambrian Mountains, but they attract much contemporary comment. Reservoirs in the Elan Valley and at Llyn Brianne have led to the adoption of the idea of this part of the Cambrian Mountains as the 'Welsh Lakeland' and descriptions of these areas feature in recent tourism promotional literature; for example, 'the beautiful lakelands of Mid-Wales, a series of spectacular reservoirs high in remote and previously inaccessible hill country'. Opinions as to the landscape merits of the reservoirs appear to vary. *The Shell Guide to Wales* suggests that the Elan Valley reservoirs 'seem to fit into the landscape' (5) whereas Timothy Porter finds them 'dull and tasteless', even 'downright hideous' (8).

Forestry plantations have been the subject of even more controversy. Lovers of the wild, desert-like qualities of the high moorlands are outraged by the alien intrusion of forests on the open landscape. *The Shell Guide to Wales* comments on how forestry plantations modify the sense of wild loneliness and how ultimately the whole ecology of the area will be altered by 'the scars made by the new Forestry Commission roads and the terraced insets in which are planted the infant firs' (5). Sale refers to the 'ranks of conifers' as pollutants (7). By contrast, some contemporary tourist guides and promotional literature describe forests as one of the visitor resources of the area, suggesting for example that you can 'lose yourself amidst deep forests, plunging down to sheer stretches of water', and describing the attractions of forest visitor centres and forest walks and trails.

"...partly cultivated, partly covered with wood, and here and there dotted with farmhouses and gentlemen's seats; green pastures which descended nearly to the river..."

George Borrow, *Wild Wales*, 1862

"...foam, foam, foam is flying all about you (enough to) haunt you through life..."

George Borrow, *Wild Wales*, 1862

"For the modern wayfarer, it is all of these horrid, frightful things that are so attractive and he can handle them in quantities in excess of one per day."

Richard Sale, *A Cambrian Way*, 1983

"It must be admitted that these grey walls of heavy stone seem to fit into the landscape, and the lakes behind them are glorious when full to the brim after rain ... the first dam is Caban Coch, built at a narrow part of the valley with impressive crags and tree clad hill-sides all around."

W. Vaughan Thomas, *The Shell Guide to Wales*, 1969

Perception of the landscape today

The landscape is perceived differently by groups of people; each having a unique view of their own surroundings. The main groups who, we suggest, may have materially different views of the landscape are:

- those who live in the area and rely on management of the land for their day to day living (especially farmers and foresters);
- those who live in or near the area and regard it as simply a part of their local environment (there are likely to be differences in opinion between long term residents and newcomers);
- those who come to the area as car-borne visitors generally wishing to enjoy the scenery, but not necessarily with any specific interest or activity in mind;
- those who come to take part in active outdoor pursuits, including hill walkers and pony trekkers;
- those who have a particular interest in and knowledge of specific aspects of the environment, such as the flora and fauna.

Farmers and foresters make their living from the land and are consequently likely to see beauty in well managed and productive ground, much as the improvers of previous centuries admired efforts to tame the wild areas. Some information on farmers' attitudes is available from the results of interviews carried out in the parish of Ysbyty Ystwyth as part of the Countryside Commission's *Upland Landscapes Study* (11).

Of 26 farmers in the parish, nearly all could name places in the immediate area which particularly appealed to them. The valley of the Ystwyth was much loved, as was the Hafod Estate, and the variety of trees, summer vegetation and contrast of valley and mountain with farm and forest were all found to be pleasing. There appears to have been a recognition of change taking place and a view that this was generally for the better. Nearly all the farmers recognised that farming was important to the landscape, many of them mentioning the importance of maintaining and improving the land. One farmer said that he would 'plough at a loss to maintain the quality of the land'.

We have no evidence concerning the views of those involved in forestry, but we would expect that they also would emphasise the merits of improvement and positive management.

Local residents are unlikely to have consistent views on the landscape. Some may be so familiar with the area that they pay little attention to the landscape. Some will make active use of the area for leisure and recreation and have a special knowledge of certain areas. Others, especially those involved in tourism, are likely to be aware of the value of the landscape to visitors. Interestingly, though, in informal conversations with local residents in Llanwrtyd Wells, we heard fairly consistent views expressed about the unwelcome effects of new forestry in the area.

Car-borne and day visitors tend to enjoy the scenery mainly from cars or coaches and are likely to be attracted by well publicised beauty spots. Indirect evidence about known beauty spots, scenic routes, viewpoints and visitor attractions helps to indicate which places are particularly popular and how this group of visitors might perceive the landscape of the Cambrian Mountains. Specific tourist attractions are the gorges and falls at Devil's Bridge, the Rheidol Railway, the ruins of the Cistercian Abbey at Strata Florida, the Rheidol Forest Visitor Centre, Llywernog Mine and the Hafren Forest walks.

A large proportion of car-borne visitors see the landscape from the A44, which is the main route through the centre of the area, running from Llangurig to Aberystwyth. A number of routes are known

"I must confess I find (the dams) dull and tasteless and the Caban Coch dams downright hideous. The landscape hereabouts is rocky and precipitous and at one time the Elan Valley must have been a most impressive and beautiful place."

T. Porter, *'Elenith'*

"...most thought that their re-seeding had made the countryside greener and thus better to look at."

Farmers of Ysbyty Yswyth Parish, *Uplands Landscapes Study: Parish Report on Ysbyty Yswyth*

"Quite a few mentioned ... that new forestry was now growing which, on the whole, was found to be an improvement."

Farmers of Ysbyty Yswyth Parish, *Uplands Landscapes Study: Parish Report on Ysbyty Yswyth*

"...still the preserve of a devoted minority, upland scenery has gained popularity with accessibility from the cities, with the taste for hiking and with increasing scarcity of lowland recreation sites owing to agriculture and other development."

D. Lowenthal, *Finding Valued Landscapes*, 1978

Extensive plateau moorland

Deep wooded valleys

Important wildlife habitats

The traditional features that give the Cambrian Mountains landscape its outstanding value.

Wilderness qualities

and signposted as scenic routes, notably the minor road from Staylittle via Dylife to Machynlleth across the northern escarpment, the old drover's road from Tregaron to Abergwesyn and the road from Rhayader through Cwmystwyth.

Water is a major attraction for visitors, and the area of reservoirs in the Cambrian Mountains has become known as the 'Lakeland of Wales'. The Elan Valley Visitor Centre receives a large number of tourists and day visitors from the east, particularly the Midlands. A survey carried out in 1986 (12) suggests that many visitors come to see the dams and the reservoirs themselves, drawn by the picturesque mixture of steep, rocky, heather-clad slopes and mixed woodlands, and the dramatic stone dams and spillway systems. Llyn Brianne is also very popular, particularly with day visitors from Swansea. The main attractions here are reported to be the quality of the landscape and opportunities for a peaceful drive in the countryside (13).

Groups involved in active recreation tend to seek out the wildness of the central moorland. The most common pursuit is hiking, but other activities are growing in popularity. Pony trekkers ride from centres such as Rhayader and Llanwrtyd Wells, mountain bikers are increasingly using the hills and orienteering takes place in the Hafren Forest.

There are a number of unofficial long-distance footpaths across the area, such as the Cambrian Way, Glyndwr's Way (which the Countryside Commission now proposes to designate as an official national trail) and the Wye Valley Walk. Books describing these footpath routes give an indication of the type of country which is favoured. Those on the Cambrian Way, for example, emphasise the contrast between picturesque valleys and wild, open moorland. In addition to these routes, much of the central moorland area of the Elenydd has a general right of access under the provisions relation to the Birmingham Corporation's Elan Valley water catchment area. These provide a right of 'air, exercise and recreation' over large areas of these wild, open grass moorlands. This area, perhaps more than most, provides everything that the wilderness lover seeks; severe terrain, vast open spaces and difficult conditions.

This particular taste for moorlands has been further examined in a number of studies. Marian Shoard (14) interviewed a number of people active in the cause of promoting access to moorland, and found that they had a passion for wilderness, openness, unrestricted access and rough, undulating, irregular upland terrain which is considered to be largely devoid of signs of the hand of man. A survey conducted by David Shimwell (15) into the attitudes of a group of 39 professionals involved in landscape also identified a similar image of moorland. Adjectives used to describe such landscapes included evaluative words, notably windy, beautiful, wet, bleak, desolate, lonely, peaceful, powerful, fresh, harsh and quiet; spatial words such as open, extensive, spacious, expansive, and empty; scenic words including wild, rolling, eroded, rough, barren, hilly, misty, rocky; words relating to access, namely remote, isolated and high; and emotive words such as invigorating, challenging, and inspiring.

Special interest groups are attracted to the Cambrian Mountains for a variety of reasons, notably interest in birds and historic features such as the ancient drove roads. Birds are a particular attraction because of the rare habitats which survive for raptors such as the Red Kite. We met a number of people who were visiting the moorlands and valleys specifically in the hope of seeing these birds.

People who have these special interests tend to view landscape in a particular way. They have knowledge which enables them to read different meanings into what other people would regard purely as scenery and they are drawn to areas where their interests are best represented.

"Only parts of the Scottish Highlands can vie with (the Cambrian Mountains) for wildness ... I will never forget my first sight of the Elenith ... Since then I have had many adventures on foot ... but it has never lost for me this atmosphere of half concealed malignance, on dark days when nothing stirs on the tops. On sunny, breezy days, everything can seem gentle and sweet, but the smile is elegiac rather than carefree."

T. Porter, 'Elenith'

"The thing about the moorland area is the feeling that ... you can walk anywhere. You have access to everywhere you can see ... it's like going into the picture ... You can actually go in and you can possess it."

C. Harrison, Recreation 2000. Views of the Country from the City, 1986

5. The importance of the Cambrian Mountains landscape

A consensus on a highly valued landscape

The high landscape quality of the Cambrian Mountains has been recognised for many years, and officially since the mid-1940s when both the Dower and Hobhouse reports suggested the area for designation. The area, originally identified in two separate parts as Plynlimon and the Elenith (or in Welsh Elenydd) Mountains, was listed as a reserve area for a national park in John Dower's 1945 report and as a Conservation Area in the 1947 Hobhouse Report.

In 1972 the Countryside Commission considered the landscape to be of such high quality that it was designated as the Cambrian Mountains National Park. At that time the Secretary of State for Wales declined to confirm the designation. However, concern for the conservation of the landscape of the area remained. In 1986 the Commission and the Nature Conservancy Council proposed that the area should be designated as the Cambrian Mountains Environmentally Sensitive Area (ESA). This designation was made in two stages, but now the whole area covered by this report is an ESA, recognising not only its landscape value but also its wildlife and archaeological interest, and the fact that the maintenance of these values is dependent upon traditional farming activities.

The detailed boundaries which have been drawn over the years, for the Hobhouse Conservation area, the proposed national park and the current ESA, all vary to some degree, but they all encompass the same core area of moorland, moorland margins, valleys, and gorges that lie at the heart of what makes the Cambrian Mountains landscape so special. There is therefore an informed consensus, which has been consistently maintained over the years, that this landscape is of national importance.

An important type of landscape

The value of the Cambrian Mountains today is to a large extent due to the particular type of landscape that they represent. There are few other places in England or Wales that combine such a large extent of rolling, uninterrupted plateau moorland with the contrasting, but equally striking features of deep, wooded valleys, river gorges and dramatic escarpments. The Cambrian Mountains have more semi-natural moorland vegetation in proportion to their total area than seven of the other existing national parks, about the same amount as Snowdonia and less than only the Yorkshire Dales and Northumberland. In terms of the actual extent of moorland vegetation, the Cambrian Mountains are exceeded only by Snowdonia, the Yorkshire Dales and the Lake District. This extensive moorland, combined with the unusual and complex plateau landform, in itself gives the area special value.

Scenic quality

The Cambrian Mountains also possess an abundance of the landscape features whose presence has consistently been shown to be linked with high scenic quality – notably rough, uncultivated vegetation, bare rock, steep slopes, upland character, a variety of woodland and water, in rivers, lakes and reservoirs. We believe that the area does indeed have high scenic quality but that this quality is most evident in certain landscape types which consistently evoke a strong and positive response, usually because they have a consistent and recognisable landscape image. Particular combinations of topography and vegetation create striking effects of landform, colour, texture, scale, diversity and balance in these landscapes. This is particularly true of the landscape types which combine the traditional landscape elements, notably the open moorland plateaux, the dramatic gorges, ravines and escarpment, and the narrow, steep-sided oakwood valleys. However, it is also true of some of the newer landscapes, especially forested valleys and reservoirs, such as Llyn Brianne.

Public preference

There is no clear evidence available to indicate public preferences for the different types of landscape or indeed for the landscape of the Cambrian Mountains as a whole. Views will undoubtedly vary widely between those living in the area and those visiting it for leisure; between those who make a living from the land and those who do not; and between those who actively enjoy the bleak, open moorlands and those who prefer the shelter and domesticity of the woods, fields and valleys.

It is clear that the area is a popular destination for visitors, albeit a less well known destination than the more mountainous areas of Snowdonia to the north and the Brecon Beacons to the south. The scenery is especially important to visitors, for most of whom the main form of enjoyment is simply driving for pleasure, taking in the landscape, stopping at viewpoints and lay-bys and taking short walks. Panoramic viewpoints on the escarpment or overlooking fringe valleys, open moorlands where they are crossed by roads, reservoirs, river valleys, woodlands, and forests, waterfalls and gorges, are all popular features. Some of the most popular scenic destinations are Devil's Bridge, the Elan Valley reservoirs, Llyn Brianne, Llyn Clywedog, the Cothi, Tywi and Llyfnant Valleys and Cwm Einion (Artist's Valley) as well as the mountain roads across the moorland.

Wilderness qualities

The Cambrian Mountains undoubtedly have special value because of the illusion of 'wilderness' which is created by the open plateau moorlands. What remains of 'the great Welsh desert' is bleak, exposed, remote, inhospitable and sometimes tedious in both its extent and the difficulty of conditions underfoot. While those who appreciate this type of landscape may not be in the majority, there is little doubt that as so many other areas of mountain and moorland become ever more popular and well visited, the Cambrian Mountains will provide an increasingly valuable sanctuary of solitude and remoteness, and will continue to be seen as a haven for lovers of such wild land.

Other values

The importance of the Cambrian Mountains landscape is enhanced by the value of the area for other heritage interests. Wildlife, archaeological and historical sites and geological or geomorphological features all make major contributions to the character of the landscape, as well as having conservation value in their own right.

The Cambrian Mountains contain a wide range of important wildlife habitats supporting a great diversity of plants and animals. Sites of Special Scientific Interest cover some 25% of the area, and incorporate three National Nature Reserves, a number of County Wildlife Trust reserves and reserves owned by the Royal Society for the Protection of Birds. The bird population is especially important as the area supports almost the entire British population of Red Kite as well as other notable species including Merlin, Buzzard, Raven, Dunlin and Golden Plover.

A variety of archaeological and historical remains also occur in the area, ranging from early prehistoric funerary and settlement monuments to eighteenth and nineteenth century remains of lead mining. Areas of ancient landscape, including field systems, enclosures, burial mounds, cairns and standing stones, are particularly found on the high plateaux. There are 81 scheduled ancient monuments in the area and over 500 unscheduled archaeological sites.

The whole region is of geological, physiographical and geomorphological interest. There are many sites which demonstrate aspects of river capture, faulting, and glacial features such as glaciated valleys, cirques carved by ice, and gorges formed by snow accumulation, all of which are important features of the landscape. The area is famous for its contribution to the development of geological knowledge. Pioneers of stratigraphical geology worked in mid-Wales in the nineteenth century, and it has been said that no area of this size in the world has had such an influence upon the advancement of geological science.

Significance of landscape types

The Cambrian Mountains consist of two broad, contrasting types of area; one where land management practices have intensified in recent years, creating 'new' landscapes where traditional landscape features have increasingly given way to new features of improved upland grazing, post and wire fencing, coniferous shelterbelts and forestry plantations; the other where traditional landscapes still survive relatively intact, notably in the high, rolling moorland plateaux of the central areas, in valleys where a complex of small-scale inbye land, deciduous woodland on valley sides and rough unimproved grazing on ridges and slopes, still remains, and in escarpments, gorges and waterfalls.

It is the traditional landscapes which led to the initial identification of the Cambrian Mountains as being worthy of national park status. For example, a paper to the National Parks Commission in 1962 stated:

> "Recurring emergence has meant that rivers have been rejuvenated more than once, carving out superb gorges and fine waterfalls. Their valleys and the wide sweeps of moorland plateaux into which they are cut are the basic and complementary factors in the beauty of Mid-Wales".

The more recent recommendation for ESA status cited 'the substantial areas of semi-natural rough grazing' and 'the valley side oakwoods', coupled with 'the complexity of land form' as the landscape basis for the proposal.

These landscapes have been consistently reduced in extent during the past forty years. Those areas which remain therefore assume even greater importance by virtue of their increasing rarity. These are the landscapes which give the Cambrian Mountains their special identity and character. They also embrace many of the landscapes which have the greatest apparent appeal to local visitors and to tourists. The landscape types where these traditional features are best represented are:

- irregular upland/peaks and knobs (Plynlimon, Teifi Pools);
- plateau tops with moorland (Elenydd, Drysgol and Mallaen);
- shallow rolling plateaux with moorland (Glaslyn, Creignant Mawr);
- plateau margins/cliffs and cirques (Dulas and Pont Marteg);
- gorges and ravines (Devil's Bridge);
- V-shaped valleys with moorland and with reservoirs (Claerwen, Craig Goch, Nant-y-moch, Cwm Ystwyth);
- V-shaped valleys with broadleaved woodland (Dinas).

Other landscape types which are also important because of their scenic quality and popularity with visitors are the V-shaped valleys, with mixed woodland, forests or reservoirs, and the U-shaped fringe valleys.

A nationally important landscape

The Cambrian Mountains landscape has long been recognised as being of national importance, with its combination of extensive tracts of rolling, uninterrupted plateau moorland and the contrasting features of deep wooded valleys, river gorges and dramatic escarpments. These features, combined with some of the newer forest and reservoir landscapes, create a landscape of high scenic quality which makes an important contribution to the enjoyment of visitors to the area. The 'wilderness' qualities of the open moorland plateaux, offering solitude and remoteness, are particularly important, and the significance of the area for wildlife, archaeology and geological and geomorphological interest further enhances its landscape value.

The landscape types which combine the traditional features of moorland and deciduous woodland with the complex landforms of plateau, valley, gorge and escarpment are most important in giving the Cambrian Mountains their special character and sense of place.

The landscape is much changed from the days when designation as a national park was first considered, when there was such an extent of uninterrupted moorland and such an intricate network of contrasting valleys. Nevertheless, there are still sufficient areas which retain this character to suggest that the landscape remains of national importance, and is on a par with other designated upland areas in both national parks and areas of outstanding natural beauty. The wilderness and solitude of much of the great Welsh desert remains to inspire us today as it has others in the past:

> "It is a country of great open landscapes. On clear days there are few places where the eye can range so widely or can follow the swiftly moving cloud shadows or the flights of numerous buzzards so far as from the summit of Plynlimon."

Margaret Davies, to the National Parks Commission, 1962.

Acknowledgements

Thanks are due to Alan Rugman and Jo Meredith of the Countryside Commission for their support and encouragement with this work.

We are grateful to Martin Parry and Geoffrey Sinclair for providing detailed information on land use, vegetation and change in the area, and to Jim Cowie of ADAS in Aberystwyth for providing additional information on land use and vegetation in the extended area of the ESA.

The National Library of Wales provided access to a large volume of reference material about the area. Kyffin Williams and Ian Mayes kindly gave permission to reproduce the painting of Teifi Pools.

Photographs are by Colin Horseman, Geoff Sinclair and Land Use Consultants. The study team was Carys Swanwick, Kim Wilkie, Mark Adams and Branwen Parry Jones, with assistance from Geoff Sinclair of Environment Information Services.

References

(1)   Defoe, D A *Tour Through the Whole Island of Great Britain, Letter 6 – The West and Wales*, 1724–26.

(2)   Pennant, T, *Tours in Wales*, Volume 3, Humphreys, 1883.

(3)   Borrow, G, *Wild Wales*, Collins, 1862.

(4)   Bradley, A G, *Mid-Wales Guidebook*, A & C Black, 1910.

(5)   Vaughan T W, and Llewellyn A, *The Shell Guide to Wales*, Michael Joseph, 1969.

(6)   Fishlock, T, *Wales and the Welsh*, Cassell, 1972.

(7)   Sale, R A *Cambrian Way*, Constable & Co., 1983.

(8)   Porter, T, *Elenith*, Youth Hostels Association (undated).

(9)   Condry, W, *Exploring Wales*, Faber, 1970.

(10) Davies, M, *Another national park*, 1972.

(11) Sinclair, G et al, *Upland Landscapes Study: Parish Report on Ysbyty Ystwyth*, (unpublished report).

(12) McBride, A, *Report on the Elan Valley Visitors Survey*, unpublished report, 1986.

(13) Llyn Brianne Working Party, *Llyn Brianne Development and Management Progress*, unpublished report, 1975.

(14) Shoard, M, 'The Lure of the Moors', in Gold and Burgess (eds), *Valued Environments*, George Allen and Unwin, 1982.

(15) Shimwell, D, 'Images of Moorland', *Recreation Ecology Research Group Conference*, Report No. 8, 1982.

Appendix 1: the method for assessing the Cambrian Mountain landscape

Introduction

In devising a method we were guided by the detailed requirements of the brief which suggested that the work should involve:

(i) the identification and description of different types of landscape in a systematic way;

(ii) the identification of areas within each different type of landscape according to their quality and value as landscape;

(iii) an assessment of the value of the different types of landscape one to another;

(iv) the identification of different areas of each landscape type according to their vulnerability to change.

The method was influenced by the time available, the extent and complexity of the area and the purpose of the assessment, as well as by our experience elsewhere and knowledge of alternative approaches. It consisted of two basic steps.

(i) Analysis of the nature of the landscape and its classification into landscape types. This was based on a combination of map work and field survey, with the two procedures complementing and informing each other. For example, direct observation of landform and vegetation in the field helped to interpret the relative importance of map information on these aspects. Similarly, subtle variations in land use or vegetation noted in the field, were explained by reference to maps. The essential elements covered by the analysis were:

- Landform, defined by combinations of slope and elevation, which produce the shape and form of the ground surface, i.e. the 'skeleton' of the landscape.
- Land cover, defined by combinations of land use and vegetation, to characterise the 'skin' that covers the landform skeleton.

(ii) When landscape types were defined we reviewed the ways in which they might be perceived, drawing on a range of evidence and including our own responses.

Analysis and classification of the landscape

After a preliminary site visit, the first major area of work was to prepare a series of map overlays in order to draw out the relationship between landform and land cover.

Landform mapping

Analysis of landform was based on the OS 1:50,000 Landranger maps. The initial field visit had suggested that plateaux, valleys and margins would be the main kinds of landform of significance. Landform mapping had to be designed to reveal these types clearly. Two overlays were prepared. One showed broad elevation categories of 0–250 m, 250–450 m and over 450 m, and steep slopes of greater than 1:4. This helped to delineate the broad, rolling plateau areas as distinct from the intervening system of valleys. The other overlay showed river drainage systems and watershed ridge lines, and helped to show the valley systems clearly. These two overlays helped to produce a simplified landform units map, which divided the area into plateaux, valleys and margin areas that are likely to be perceived differently on the ground.

Land cover mapping

The *Mid Wales uplands study* had collected 1983 land use information which had been updated by field work in 1985. This was used to produce a tracing overlay showing the distribution of improved pasture, rough grazing, broadleaved woodland, mixed woodlands and forest and water.

As a result of the preliminary site visit we concluded that further detail of the nature and distribution of semi-natural vegetation would be of value in the assessment. Our view was that the contrasting textures and seasonally varying colours of moorland vegetation are important features of the area. Detailed, though not up to date, information was available, but the pattern of vegetation types was extremely complex. This information was simplified to provide information which could more easily be interpreted in overlay form.

All the information on land use and semi-natural rough grazing was then overlayed and a composite map produced showing simplified land cover zones, based on the land cover type which was most extensive and likely to be visually dominant. Overlaying the landform and land cover maps allowed a complete 'bird's-eye' view of the landscape to be built up, and patterns identified.

Field survey

Formal observations were made at a number of observation points, which were selected in relation to our first approximation of landscape types. Observations were made from roads, footpaths and other publicly accessible points. The same procedures were followed at each point and were designed to make the surveyors look clearly and consistently at the landscape visible from each point, and to record its salient features.

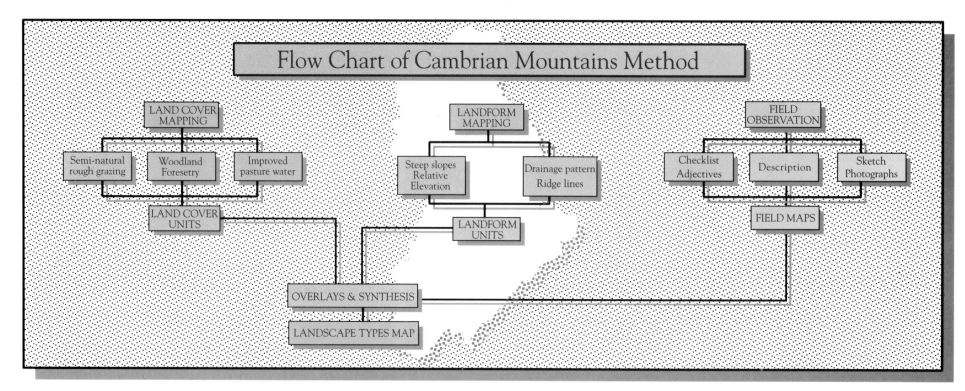

Flow Chart of Cambrian Mountains Method

LAND COVER MAPPING
- Semi-natural rough grazing
- Woodland Foresetry
- Improved pasture water

LAND COVER UNITS

LANDFORM MAPPING
- Steep slopes Relative Elevation
- Drainage pattern Ridge lines

LANDFORM UNITS

FIELD OBSERVATION
- Checklist Adjectives
- Description
- Sketch Photographs

FIELD MAPS

OVERLAYS & SYNTHESIS

LANDSCAPE TYPES MAP

The procedures were:

(i) write a brief description of the landscape, noting the overall impression, key features and so on;

(ii) make a quick illustrative sketch of the landscape, again with a view to highlighting the main features;

(iii) complete a checklist of landscape elements, indicating whether they are inconspicuous, evident, or very conspicuous, and also showing the nature of views and any specific observations on land use or activities;

(iv) complete a checklist to indicate subjective impressions of the landscape using a series of adjectives;

(v) take a series of photographs.

These procedures were not designed to provide information for any form of quantitative analysis, but to ensure consistent and thorough appraisal of the landscape at each point. The sketches and brief descriptions proved to be particularly helpful in this respect. The checklists used were not intended to be followed absolutely rigorously, but to act as an *aide memoire*. Other elements, words or annotations were added as appropriate.

Division into landscape types

Once the fieldwork was complete, a lengthy process of information sorting and analysis took place. Review of the series of landform and land cover overlay maps, together with the annotated field maps and the observation records, allowed areas of similar character to be identified and grouped together into landscape types. This 'clustering' process was complex and many rough versions were produced before the final map of landscape types emerged.

The process relied to some extent on intuitive judgements as well as on rational analysis of all the information. Divisions of landscape into, for example, small-scale or large-scale valleys, or rolling or irregular plateaux, is a matter, in our method, of judgement rather than of measurement. Other interpretations could have been put on the information, but the results, set out in this report, appear to be a fair reflection of the nature of the landscape. The descriptions of landscape types are based on a compilation of evidence from both map overlays and field survey. The process for defining landscape types is summarised in the flow diagram.

Perception of the landscape

Our approach to this part of the study was to draw upon as wide a range of evidence as possible, in order to throw light upon the way in which the landscape is perceived. This evidence included:

(i) our own judgements, made at individual field survey points, about the perceptual qualities of the different landscape types in the study area;

(ii) written descriptions, and artistic impressions of the area, which give an indication of the way in which people who are inspired by this landscape have reacted to it over time;

(iii) evidence, both direct and indirect, of the way in which different groups of people perceive this landscape today;

(iv) evidence from other sources and other studies about the way in which landscape of this type is generally perceived.

Our own judgements

In the field survey we made provision for recording our own subjective perceptions of the different landscapes. We developed a checklist of 75 descriptive adjectives, arranged within 15 ranges of extremes. The list was drawn up in advance, after the first field visit, to cover the factors which we felt were most likely to be relevant for this type of landscape. They covered characteristics such as openness or enclosure, wildness, level of disturbance, harmony, and so on. Other adjectives were added whenever the list appeared inadequate in the field.

The procedure in the field was to complete the checklist at each observation point as quickly as possible in order to capture an immediate response and to attempt to standardise the level of attention given to each point. The checklist was completed jointly by the two surveyors. Where their responses disagreed there was discussion as to why this might be and resolution of the disagreement. This generally happened in transitional areas between landscape types, or in areas which did not have particularly strong landscape character.

The results of this subjective assessment formed part of the field survey records and were used in categorising the landscape types, in description of the types and in consideration of perception of the landscape.

Other sources

Evidence about the way others perceive the landscape can be gleaned from a variety of sources. Written sources include eighteenth and nineteenth century discourses on particular areas, technical reports, guidebooks, contemporary tourist literature and official files, as well as other landscape studies. We were able to review a number of the most relevant sources over a period spent in the National Library of Wales in Aberystwyth, which revealed an extensive range of material about the area.

We had hoped to be able to review the Countryside Commission's original national park designation files. These proved to be unavailable, but we did have access to the personal files of one of the Commissioners most actively involved at the time when designation was proposed, and this provided useful information about what the particular merits of the landscape were considered to be.

This type of research can be extremely time-consuming and a balance has to be struck between reviewing every possible source and reviewing only those which appear to be most relevant, thereby running the risk of being too selective. We attempted to continue with the research until the information we were gathering began to reveal a clear pattern about the way in which the landscape was perceived, and until we had reasonable coverage of different historical periods, different groups of people and different areas or features of the landscape.

Once the landscape types had been identified, mapped and described, and once research on perception of these landscapes had been completed, we were able to review all this, and other relevant information, to make judgements about the value and importance of the landscape as a whole and of the landscape types within it.

Wider applicability of the method

Over the past five years there has been a move away from attempts at evaluation of landscape quality towards a recognition that landscape character can be equally important. Policies, whether concerning development, land use or land management, can be designed to maintain the particular characteristics of individual areas and therefore help to maintain the 'sense of place' which is so important to the British countryside. Assessment of landscape character is a key part of this process and the method used in this study should have wider applicability in other areas.

The method, however, must be tailored to the area in question and to the problem being addressed. In lowland areas, for example, there is likely to be less emphasis, when determining landscape types, on landform and more on, for example, field size, or historical evolution of the landscape. Emphasis on character does not do away with the need for judgements about the relative value of landscapes. The method used here is based on the belief that there is no such thing as a single universal value system for landscape. There is therefore a need to draw upon as wide as possible a range of evidence about the values which are attached to a particular landscape by different groups of people, and about the way in which they perceive the landscape. Information about the landscape preferences of different groups of people is in short supply and the picture is inevitably, therefore, somewhat incomplete. Professional judgement of landscape value is one part of this assessment, but must be set alongside the other evidence which is available. This approach appears to be finding greater favour at present than are attempts at quantitative landscape evaluation.

Responses to the method

The method of landscape assessment used was commented upon by those involved with land use issues in the area, notably officers of the Forestry Commission and the Ministry of Agriculture Fisheries and Food (MAFF). MAFF (ADAS) commented upon the value of the approach for monitoring the Environmentally Sensitive Area and found it did not entirely meet their specific requirements. In summary they felt that the approach of dividing landscape types hierarchically – first on the basis of landform and then on the basis of land cover, was not ideal – and that a process which aimed simply to define areas of homogeneous character would be preferable. In later comments on use of the method in considering forestry in the landscape, the ADAS landscape advisor indicated that the general methodology for defining landscape types was well tested and worked well in this example.

The Forestry Commission commented that the method was ambiguous in dealing with perception, because it mixed the consultant's view with the views of other groups and individuals. It was also felt that the opinions quoted were heavily biased to those groups who are predictably antagonistic to change and that other views should have been equally represented, even if this meant carrying out additional attitude research.